Pre-College Programming in Higher Education

The Evolution of a Movement

A practitioner's handbook for
current and future pre-college programming leaders

Edited by
Susan L. Sheth, Ph.D.
and
Christopher W. Tremblay, Ed.D.

© 2019
Published by Kindle Direct Publishing
Cover Design by Christopher W. Tremblay and Susan Sheth

ISBN 9781794134041

Praise for the Book

"This is a text that is critically needed for practitioners in and students of pre-college programming. Sheth and Tremblay take a holistic view of the value of K-12 programming in higher education; this is critically important in the face of shifting demographics and the ongoing need to engage with students earlier and more intentionally than ever before. The dimensions of pre-college programming offer a thoughtful and comprehensive framework for universities to seriously consider."

Elena Ragusa, Psy.D.
Director of Strategic Initiatives
Division of Enrollment Management
Rutgers University–New Brunswick

"Because of the current realities in higher education, there are implications for institutional policies and practices which include the need for pre-college programs. Through this book, the reader is introduced to various concepts such as Kolb's Experimental Learning Theory, laws that protect minors, and case studies. I would highly recommend this one-of-a-kind book to higher education colleagues."

Kimberley Buster-Williams, Ed.S.
Vice President for Enrollment Management
University of Mary Washington

Acknowledgements

Thank you to our 16 contributing authors who dedicated time and energy to share their expertise for this book.

Thank you to University Outreach and Engagement at Michigan State University for granting permission to reprint William Edwards' seminal article on pre-college programming.

Thank you to William Edwards for granting permission to reprint his article on pre-college programming.

Thank you to Burt Bargerstock, Director, National Collaborative for the Study of University Engagement, for his support of this publication.

Thank you to Julie Rickert for editing and typesetting this book, along with checking sources.

About the Co-Editors

Susan Sheth, Ph.D.

Dr. Susan Sheth is the director of Gifted and Talented Education (GATE) at Michigan State University. Prior to her time at MSU, Susan taught communications at the University of Michigan for 12 years before pursuing gifted education. Her pursuits for the gifted include creating more opportunities, building stronger educational curricula, and identification of gifted students. Susan received her Ph.D. from the University of Toledo in Curriculum and Instruction of Gifted Education. Sheth is currently the president of the Michigan Association for Gifted Children and is Northwestern University's Midwest Academic Talent Search Program liaison for southeast and mid-Michigan. Her goals at GATE include offering gifted programming for underserved populations and expanding opportunities throughout the state of Michigan. Since joining MSU, some notable additions to GATE include hosting the Michigan Association for Gifted Children state conference and collaborating with the MSU Osteopathic Hospital to create a Future DOCs-GATE summer program for middle school students, as well as expanding academic year programs into southeast Michigan. She created GUPPY (Gifted University for Parents and Precocious Youth), in which parents and young gifted students participate in on-campus learning. GATE programs began to include summer program options for students in grades 3 through 10. Susan has presented at the Michigan Association for Gifted Children and nationally at the National Association for Gifted Children, Lilly Teaching Conference and the Engagement Scholarship Consortium Pre-College Pre-Conference Workshop.

Christopher W. Tremblay, Ed.D.

Dr. Christopher W. Tremblay is Director of External Engagement for the Michigan College Access Network (MCAN). He previously worked at the University of Wisconsin-Superior, Western Michigan University, the University of Michigan-Dearborn, and Gannon University in various leadership roles. Tremblay earned both his bachelor's and master's degrees from Western Michigan University. He has a Doctor of Education in educational leadership from the University of Michigan-Dearborn. Tremblay was instrumental in the proposal and establishment of a new Office of Pre-College Programming at Western Michigan University. During his time at University of Wisconsin-Superior, he had oversight of three TRIO Programs. Tremblay serves as co-editor of the *Journal of College Access*. He has presented at more than 75 association conferences nationally and internationally, including the pre-college workshops at the Engagement Scholarship Consortium's annual conferences. Tremblay served on a special task force within the Pre-College Program Directors group. He is also the inventor of the admissions-based card game, Getting In, a tool that can be used in pre-college programs.

Chapter Contributors

Dr. William Alba
Carnegie Mellon
University

Lindsay Meyer Bond
Ohio State University

Dr. Erika Carr
Western Michigan
University

Lisa DeBenedictis
Brandeis University

William Edwards
Formerly of
Michigan State University

Dr. Meghan Groome
School of The New York
Times

Dr. Kim Lijana
University of Michigan

Kacey McCaffrey
School of The New York
Times

Dr. Candy McCorkle
Western Michigan
University

Dr. Jacqueline Newcomb
Harvard University

Susie Sheldon Rush
Carnegie Mellon
University

Dr. Kelly Schultz
Western Michigan
University

Dr. Susan Sheth
Michigan State University

Luke Steinman
Western Michigan
University

Kari Storm
Bowling Green State
University

Dr. Christopher Tremblay
Michigan College Access
Network

Table of Contents

Focus, on Perna's quotes/ data

Preface

It all started over a casual conversation in a hotel lobby in Omaha, Nebraska. We had both just presented at the Second Pre-College Pre-Conference Workshop at the Engagement Scholarship Consortium conference. Susan presented on working with diverse and underserved youth in pre-college programs. Christopher presented on his involvement in starting the Office of Pre-College Programming at Western Michigan University in Kalamazoo, Michigan.

That discussion led to the creation of a model of 25 dimensions that should exist in an ideal pre-college programming unit within higher education. Those dimensions are included in a chapter in this book. That led to a landscape review of the literature, research and models out there. That led to involvement in the Pre-College Program Directors group.

And then we decided it was time to be pioneers and document this in a handbook for colleagues and professionals in the field.

We assembled a group of talented colleagues to author these chapters. We are grateful for their contributions.

What is presented here is the first book on pre-college programming in higher education, which can also be used as a textbook and as a reference for new and veteran pre-college programming professionals.

-Susan & Christopher

Introduction

By Susan Sheth, Ph.D., Michigan State University

Although we define the variety of terms used in pre-college programming in Chapter 1, it is important to share the overview of pre-college and its potential advantages to those youth who participate. Longitudinal research has shown that college degree outcomes and career paths can be determined by the age of 13, which helps support the case of early access to a college setting for most children and their potential (Bernstein, Lubinski, & Benbow, 2019). Pre-college programs create and provide an opportunity for K-12 students to live and learn on a college campus—which is excellent early exposure to college. Pre-college programming can have a distinct mission for different universities, but most strive to provide unique experiences that are beneficial to students.

When students have the chance to "test drive" a campus, it makes them more familiar with college life and gives them confidence going forward. While on campus, students are learning in a college classroom, often interacting with a college professor, and dining in a collegiate dining hall. For residential students, they connect with undergraduate students who frequently serve as resident advisors in the residence halls. These experiences make a lasting impression on students.

It also gives students a taste of interacting with faculty and college-type learning. Doctoral-titled professors can intimidate students, but pre-college programs enable students to see how personable and knowledgeable the college faculty are. Students learn from experts in the field and are able to supplement their traditional K-12 classroom knowledge. Students often are in academic spaces like computer labs, science labs, and artist studios—where hands-on learning takes place.

Some programs may be residential and others allow students to commute from home. Examples of pre-college experiences include summer camps, gifted programs, fine arts programs, sports camps, and sometimes high school dual enrollment programs. Some programs may offer college credit and others will be available for no credit and some of these pre-college programs require tuition or a program fee.

These are educationally rich experiences, which broaden a student's horizons and facilitate interpersonal connections with their peers. For example, a student potentially interested in a STEM-related college major can jump right in and see if science, technology, engineering, and/or math is really for them.

To maximize their summer college program experience, students can choose to dabble in a variety of subject areas to explore a wide array of interests, and some universities may allow students to enter into career shadowing opportunities. This helps them determine what they like and do not like—which can assist them in the future when selecting a college major or a profession.

Overall, there can be great value in accessing pre-college programs with colleges and universities that have support from their administrators to allow for offering high quality programming.

About the Author

Dr. Susan Sheth is the director of Gifted and Talented Education (GATE) at Michigan State University. Prior to her time at MSU, Susan taught communications at the University of Michigan for 12 years before pursuing gifted education. Her pursuits for the gifted include creating more opportunities, building stronger educational curricula, and identification of gifted students. Susan received her Ph.D. from the University of Toledo in Curriculum and Instruction of Gifted Education. Sheth is currently the president of the Michigan Association for Gifted Children and is Northwestern University's Midwest Academic Talent Search Program liaison for southeast and mid-Michigan.

REFERENCE

Bernstein, B. O., Lubinski, D., & Benbow, C. P. (2019). Psychological constellations assessed at age 13 predict distinct forms of eminence 35 years later. *Psychological Science, 30*(3), 444–454. doi:10.1177/0956797618822524

Chapter 1

What is Pre-College Programming?

By Susan Sheth, Ph.D., Michigan State University and
Christopher W. Tremblay, Ed.D.,
Michigan College Access Network

One of the first concerns about developing a book about pre-college programming was to find research and develop a comprehensive history and definition of pre-college. Many of these findings will later be discussed in this book, but it is important to note that there were and are very few current books or research on this ever-growing phenomenon. This chapter details the definitions and terminology of pre-college programming while Chapter 3 provides some historical context of the pre-college evolution.

After conducting research, we found that there are very few actual definitions for pre-college. However, Merriam-Webster does define it as "occurring before college" and "not yet attending college." Within the field of education, varieties of pre-college phrases are found in use. Here we take a moment to share and define them:

Pre-College
The time period from preschool through 12th grade (P-12).

Pre-College Programming/Programs (PCP)
Programs designed for P-12 students to participate on college campuses before they become an undergraduate student.

Pre-College Outreach Programs (PCOP)

These provide educational opportunities to increase college participation for underserved populations of pre-college students. Programs help provide a pipeline for higher education opportunities to encourage and foster students who would not traditionally pursue a postsecondary education. Their mission is to increase educational opportunities and college participation for underrepresented students who are traditionally non-college bound. The use of the word "outreach" typically implies the college is making a concerted effort to "reach out" and invite students to campus.

Pre-College Intervention Programs

These programs are early programs which are designed to positively alter a student's future and inspire underserved students with the opportunity to cultivate their talents and abilities, increase their readiness for college, and to influence their postsecondary plans. They are similar to Outreach Programs.

Educational Outreach Programs

Prior to the use of the phrase "pre-college programs," educational outreach programs was the primary term. The early TRIO programs (i.e., Upward Bound) were often called educational outreach programs. Similar to Pre-College Outreach Programs (see above).

Educational Opportunity Programs

This phrase was previously used by the Council for the Advancement of Standards (CAS) for its standard for benchmarking TRIO Programs: "TRIO and Other Educational Opportunity Programs," when it was established in 1999. In 2018, it was changed to "TRIO and College Access Programs."

According to CAS:
"The mission of TRIO and College Access Programs (TCAP) must be to encourage and assist people who are traditionally underrepresented in postsecondary education because of income, family educational background, disability, or other relevant federal, state/provincial, or institutional criteria, in the preparation for, entry to, and completion of a postsecondary degree" (CAS, 2019, p. 7).

College Access Programs
These are initiatives that focus on college readiness and preparation in order to remove barriers that inhibit access/enrollment into college.

Inserting a hyphen between "pre" and "college" is more common than no hyphen, but both seem to be used interchangeably. In this book, we use the hyphen.

Pre-College Program Categories
Pre-college programs offered by colleges and universities come in all shapes and sizes, which can make it difficult to "categorize" them. This chapter offers some distinct and overlapping categories as a way of organizing the types and varieties of pre-college programs.

Many pre-college programs have a "theme." The theme might be an academic topic (i.e., math, English, biology), based on a current event (i.e., global warming, elections), or a special interest (particular sport or game).

Regardless of theme or program title, pre-college programs can be categorized into these four-primary areas:

Credit and Non-Credit Bearing	Time of Year	Sports and Athletic Programs	Camps

Credit and Non-Credit Bearing

Colleges and universities may offer credit courses, non-credit courses, or a combination of both.

Credit courses are offered for academic credit and appear on an official transcript issued by the college or university. These are typically taught by a college professor or adjunct instructor. These courses may transfer to other colleges/ universities, depending on their transfer policies.

Some colleges and universities may consider high school dual enrollment as a credit-bearing pre-college experience. Some pre-college program offices are responsible for the administration of high school dual enrollment programs.

Non-credit courses do not receive academic credit at a college or university, but will still likely charge a fee for the program. Some non-credit courses may issue a printed "certificate of completion." Non-credit courses may still be academic in nature—they just may not be taught by a college professor or meet other credit-course require-ments. Non-credit pre-college programs may also be of equal value.

Time of Year

A majority of the pre-college programs take place in the summer since that is when K-12 students have the most time available. Summer pre-college programs may be as short as one day and could be as long as several weeks. Some pre-college programs are offered during the academic year. For example, some of the programming offered by the Michigan State University Gifted and Talented Education (GATE) program takes place during the academic year. Students meet regularly throughout the semester like a college course.

Sports and Athletic Programs
While not all pre-college program practitioners agree that sports and athletic programs are considered "pre-college programs," they do exist and offer valuable experiences to the K-12 student population. They offer exposure to team-work, sports drills, competition, and leadership. These athletic programs are typically focused on one particular sport and can be treated as a "clinic." In many instances, these programs may also be referred to as "sports camps."

Camps
The use of the word "camps" in the pre-college program environment can also be controversial because "camps" can be perceived as less than academic. However, some fine arts programs, like in music, use the phrase, "music camp."

Conclusion
Although pre-college programming has many categories and definitions, there is much consistency in their establishment, yet this programming is constantly transforming to meet the needs of today's learners.

As you will see in this book, there are some common elements in the pre-college programming space, but there are also some wide variations in how this work is approached and how it is developing. Regardless of the varied models out there, many of the recommendations and practices shared by authors in this book can be applied and/or modified to meet your campus needs.

About the Authors

Dr. Susan Sheth is the director of Gifted and Talented Education (GATE) at Michigan State University. Prior to her time at MSU, Susan taught communications at the University of Michigan for 12 years before pursuing gifted education. Her pursuits for the gifted include creating more opportunities, building stronger educational curricula, and identification of gifted students. Susan received her Ph.D. from the University of Toledo in Curriculum and Instruction of Gifted Education. Sheth is currently the president of the Michigan Association for Gifted Children and is Northwestern University's Midwest Academic Talent Search Program liaison for southeast and mid-Michigan.

Dr. Christopher W. Tremblay has been active in the pre-college programming space for five years. Tremblay was instrumental in the proposal and establishment of a new Office of Pre-College Programming at Western Michigan University. During his time at the University of Wisconsin-Superior, he had oversight of three TRIO Programs. Tremblay serves as co-editor of the *Journal of College Access*. He has presented at more than 75 association conferences nationally and internationally, including the pre-college workshops at the Engagement Scholarship Consortium's annual conferences. Tremblay served on a special task force within the Pre-College Program Directors group. He currently serves as Director of External Engagement for the Michigan College Access Network (MCAN), where he serves as a member of the Michigan Pre-College and Youth Outreach Conference Steering Committee.

REFERENCE

Council for the Advancement of Standards (CAS) in Higher Education. (2019). *CAS professional standards for higher education* (10th ed.). TRIO and College Access Programs. Washington, DC: Author.

Chapter 2

Pre-College Programs and the Engaged University

By William A. Edwards,
Formerly of Michigan State University

INTRODUCTION

Pre-college programs are an important component of the engaged university's outreach mission, but are often overshadowed by the traditional research and teaching functions of the university. With increasing attention being devoted to college access issues around the country, engaged universities have an opportunity through pre-college programming to further their historical mission of reducing disparities in access to higher education. In this brief, the author describes the benefits of pre-college programming and offers suggestions for institutions to better support pre-college programs.

Until fairly recently, a high school education was sufficient training for most middle-class jobs in the United States. However, postsecondary education is critical in the knowledge-based economy of the 21st century (Drucker, 1992). As of 2006, the annual median family income of those with a four-year college degree was $50,000 more than those with a high school diploma (Haskins, Holzer, & Lerman, 2009). Despite the clear economic benefits of postsecondary education, only 39% of adult Americans hold a two- or four-year degree. Governments, foundations, and corporations in the U.S. have recognized the need to better prepare students for college in order to compete in the international economy. The engaged university, which has long promoted college access, has a significant opportunity to increase its commitment to pre-college programming to help meet the workforce demands of the knowledge-based economy.

The Kellogg Commission on the Future of State and Land-Grant Universities challenged universities to reengage with communities using collaborative practices to better align university activities with community needs (Kellogg Commission, 1999). The report specifically called on the engaged university to offer targeted academic programs to children and pre-college youth. Pre-college programs serve as a highly visible form of public engagement within the community that has the potential to "pay big dividends in the years ahead" (Kellogg Commission, 1999, p. 34).

Though the term "pre-college" is applied in many ways, the term is used broadly here to refer to campus-based college access programs. Pre-college programs can be found at postsecondary institutions across the country. They offer K-12 students opportunities to prepare academically and socially for higher education, provide a pipeline for K-12 students, and expose students to campus living and learning experiences. Higher education is heavily invested in youth outreach efforts, but the benefits of pre-college programming for the community and for the university as a whole are often overlooked. This brief describes two main types of pre-college programs, then articulates the benefits of pre-college programs to the university and the community, and finally provides suggestions to increase the role of pre-college programming on university campuses.

TYPES OF PRE-COLLEGE PROGRAMS

Two types of pre-college programs are covered here: traditional college access programs and discipline-focused programs. Traditional college access programs typically assist disadvantaged populations in preparing for college. The most widely recognized traditional college access programs are the federal TRIO programs (Swail & Perna, 2002). The acronym refers to a "trio" of three federally-funded initiatives launched in the 1960s, as part of the War on Poverty, to encourage access to higher education for low-income students. Federal appropriations for TRIO totaled over $700 million in 2008 (U.S. Department of Education [USDOE] Office of Communications and Outreach, 2008). By law, TRIO programs require at least two-thirds of the participants to be both low-income and first-generation college attendees. The remaining participants must be either low-income or first-generation. The current TRIO programs include Upward Bound, Talent Search, and GEAR UP.

Upward Bound

Upward Bound was authorized as a pilot project by the Economic Opportunity Act of 1964 to support low-income youth in graduating from high school and pursuing a college education. The program serves students between the ages of 13 and 19 who have completed the eighth grade. In the 2005-2006 academic year, Upward Bound served over 140,000 students across the country (USDOE Office of Postsecondary Education, 2008a). The program is required to offer instruction in mathematics, laboratory science, composition, literature, and foreign languages (USDOE Office of Postsecondary Education, 2008b). Programs offer an intensive summer program that simulates the college-going experience and an academic year program. During the school year, programming is usually offered on the weekend and/or after regular school hours (Calahan & Curtin, 2004).

Talent Search

Talent Search was created a year after Upward Bound as part of the Higher Education Act of 1965 to assist students applying for federal financial aid for postsecondary education. The program serves students between the ages of 11 and 27 who have completed the fifth grade. During the 2003-2004 academic year, Talent Search served approximately 400,000 participants (USDOE Office of Postsecondary Education, 2006). Services include providing information on postsecondary education, financial aid counseling, career exploration, tutorial services, exposure to college campuses, college admissions assistance, college entrance exam assistance, mentoring programs, and workshops for the families of participants. Talent Search also serves high school dropouts by encouraging them to complete their high school education and pursue postsecondary education (USDOE Office of Postsecondary Education, 2008b).

GEAR UP

GEAR UP (Gaining Early Awareness and Readiness for Undergraduate Programs) offers a wide range of services to increase the number of low-income students who are prepared to enter and succeed in postsecondary education. GEAR UP serves an entire cohort of students beginning no later than the seventh grade and follows the cohort through high school (National Council for Community and Education Partnerships, 2008). The passage of the Higher Education Opportunity Act in 2008 gives GEAR UP programs the option of continuing to serve participants during the first year of college (National Council for Community and Education Partnerships, 2008). Programs are required, at minimum, to provide financial aid counseling, encourage students to enroll in a rigorous high school curriculum, increase high school graduation rates, assist students in applying for college, and offer scholarships to participants.

In terms of academic discipline, not punishment (oops)

Very similar to AVID

Disciplinary Programs

The federal TRIO programs are the most widely known pre-college programs, but many other college access programs exist on campuses across the country. Universities sponsor a large number of programs designed to encourage interest in particular disciplines. Programs that expose students to STEM disciplines (i.e., science, technology, engineering, and mathematics) have become increasingly popular in light of government and corporate calls for more STEM graduates, a vital factor in the country's ability to compete in the global economy (Jobs for the Future, 2007). Particular emphasis has been placed on attracting more women and minority students to STEM disciplines. Discipline-focused pre-college programs can also be found in the arts, foreign language and area studies, health professions, agriculture, communications, teacher education, business, and political science. Programs may be short- or long-term, residential or commuter.

BENEFITS OF PRE-COLLEGE PROGRAMS

Benefits to Participants

Traditional K-12 schools have also incorporated programs to place students on a college-going path. However, educational stakeholders are increasingly devoting more attention to the education of children outside of the traditional school day (Jordan & Nettles, 2000). Out-of-school time (OST) programming, like pre-college, offers students enrichment opportunities outside of the classroom and provides youth with structured environments, especially during the summer months. OST programming increases the academic skills of students and assists in developing positive youth assets (Pittman, Irby, Yohalem, & Wilson-Ahlstrom, 2004). Participation in OST programming has been linked to increased efforts to complete homework, increased parental engagement (Kane, 2004), increased intrinsic motivation, more effort, less apathy, and increased positive emotions (Vandell et al., 2005). Choy, Horn, Nunez, and Chen (2000) found that college outreach programs targeting high-school students doubled the odds that students would enroll in postsecondary education.

Funding devoted to OST programming has increased substantially over the past few decades (Borman, 2001). Annual appropriations for the 21st Century Community Learning Centers, which fund a broad array of before- and after-school programs, increased from $453 million in 2001 to $981 million in 2007 (USDOE, 2008). These funding increases have doubled the availability of OST programming within the public schools over the past 25 years (Borman, 2001). Nonetheless, the demand for OST programming, including college access programming, far outpaces the supply (Fairchild & Boulay, 2002; Venezia & Rainwater, 2007).

Benefits to the Community
College access programs are not exclusively campus-based. Community-based college access programs have become a popular way to assist youth in pursuing postsecondary education. However, pre-college programs offer several unique advantages over college access programming outside the university. First, the university campus offers a wealth of expertise for youth outreach professionals.

Content and pedagogical expertise on campus is an important resource for youth outreach programs that may not always be present in other college programs. Secondly, the university has the potential to foster increased motivations toward and preparation for postsecondary education among youth (Venezia & Rainwater, 2007). Finally, because of the expertise on campus, the engaged university is uniquely situated to serve as a leader within the community on college access programming that can help other youth-serving organizations embed college access into existing programming.

Benefits to Institutions

Pre-college programming offers a number of benefits to postsecondary institutions as well. First, pre-college programming is used to recruit students and to promote specific majors. Second, with most of the undergraduate population off campus during the summer, pre-college programs serve as an important source of revenue for postsecondary institutions during the summer months.

At Michigan State University, for example, $3 million of revenue was generated by housing over 20,000 youth in 2008. More and more colleges are counting on pre-college programs to generate additional revenue during the summer months when the campus serves fewer undergraduate students (Foderaro, 2009). Finally, pre-college programs are an investment in the community. The research and teaching functions are often referenced to demonstrate the importance of postsecondary institutions to communities, but pre-college programs touch many families and are a valuable service to communities. As pressures mount to demonstrate the public good of postsecondary institutions, the contributions of pre-college programs cannot be overlooked.

SUPPORTING PRE-COLLEGE PROGRAMS

Since pre-college programs provide significant benefits to both communities and postsecondary institutions, coordinated institutional investment in such programs has the potential to yield even greater impacts. To develop systemic supports for pre-college programs, postsecondary institutions can improve organizational structures around pre-college programs and create systems to document and evaluate their impact on participants, the community, and the university.

Improving Organizational Structures

Some institutions may centralize pre-college functions, but at most universities, pre-college programs are scattered across campus. Without adequate support at the institutional level, programs may lack the resources to maintain funding and staffing. Professionals working with pre-college programs in a decentralized environment may have few opportunities to interact with other youth outreach professionals. Central organizational support can help legitimize pre-college programs on campus and offer coordination of resources to better support them. Two options that institutions might consider to increase support for pre-college programs include appointing a senior administrator to oversee pre-college functions and creating a community of practice around pre-college programming.

Central administrator.

The appropriate senior administrator or group of administrators will largely depend on the institution, but likely candidates include the senior administrators for outreach or continuing education, student support services, or enrollment management. The administrator(s) can offer general oversight and funding support to pre-college programs and serve as a point of entry for those interested in participating. Having one or more senior administrators responsible for pre-college programs has the advantage of support within the executive levels of the institution.

Communities of practice.
Although investment in a central administrator has the potential to leverage significant impacts for pre-college programs, budgetary constraints in today's environment may make it difficult to implement this option. Another—and a low-cost—option for institutions seeking to create organizational structures to support pre-college programs is to form a community of practice. Wenger, McDermott, and Snyder (2002) define a community of practice as "a group of people who share a concern, a set of problems, or a passion about a topic, and who deepen their knowledge and expertise in this area by interacting on an ongoing basis" (p. 4). Communities of practice cut across traditional organizational and disciplinary structures and can exist without any formal recognition by the institution. A community of practice around pre-college programs has the potential to foster greater expertise among pre-college professionals, more effective collaborations within the university, and improved partnerships outside of the institution.

Expertise on the university campus is invaluable. Most youth outreach programs at postsecondary institutions are still in the early stages of developing professional standards. Youth development professionals may not be educators by training and are "often unfamiliar with the literature to support their program goals and methods" (Wiltz, 2005, p. 16). Communities of practice can support pre-college professionals by sharing informational resources that will build expertise as well as by facilitating collaboration between program administrators and university faculty with expertise

in the areas of interest. Furthermore, pre-college professionals can use the community of practice to disseminate
information about program outcomes and expand awareness and investment in pre-college programs.

A community of practice around pre-college programs can
also encourage greater collaboration within the university.
With budget deficits affecting postsecondary institutions
across the country, sharing resources becomes a greater
priority. Additionally, the educational needs of youth are
evolving in many ways and programs must find ways to
respond to this evolution. Shifts in population, the economy,
the workforce, the environment, and technology all impact
how educational institutions should be preparing youth to
succeed in postsecondary education and to function as
global citizens. Just as university research and undergraduate education are beginning to move beyond traditional
disciplinary lines, pre-college programs must respond to
the complex, multi-faceted issues that affect youth by
developing initiatives that span disciplines. Multidisciplinary efforts are likely to be more appealing to funders and
will allow practitioners to approach these complex issues
from different disciplinary traditions.

Finally, a community of practice around pre-college programs can foster better collaboration with community
organizations. When pre-college programs are scattered
across the university, each program's personnel is responsible for their own networking, with varying success
depending on the individuals and units involved. However,
a community of practice creates a platform for pre-college
directors to share their external networks and promote
each other's programs.

Documenting and Evaluating the Impact of Pre-College Programs

With reform efforts sweeping K-12 education systems and increasing pressure for accountability on higher education from governments and the public, precollege programs must establish systems to measure program outcomes and impacts. The intended outcomes of traditional K-12 education, especially since No Child Left Behind, have tended to rely on standardized tests and grades. These measures of success stand in sharp contrast to the intended outcomes of many pre-college programs, which focus on building developmental assets and preparing students for college.

Despite increasing investment in pre-college programs, little is known about the outcomes and effectiveness of these programs (Swail & Perna, 2002). Even the federal TRIO programs and other large-scale pre-college programs lack significant longitudinal data on program outcomes. Many pre-college programs lack sufficient funding to conduct evaluations. Moreover, program directors may not see assessment and evaluation as particularly relevant to helping students get into college (Tierney, 2002), instead preferring to devote all funds to programming. However, with increased expectations among funders for demonstrated outcomes, pre-college programs must develop systems to measure their impact.

Individual pre-college programs have limited resources and generally lack expertise in assessment and evaluation. To address these needs, postsecondary institutions can create centralized systems to measure program outcomes (Swail & Perna, 2002). Documenting participants' subsequent college enrollment and graduation rates is a practice that should be applied to all pre-college programs. The National Student Clearinghouse is a national enrollment verification system that can be used by pre-college programs to determine college enrollment and graduation rates for program participants. The system provides detailed information for each student, including postsecondary institutions attended.

However, most pre-college programs have established outcomes that go beyond enrollment and graduation. Other program outcomes may include increased motivation for postsecondary education, interest in particular fields, interest in a particular institution, increased motivation toward K-12 education, improved college transitions, increases in specific content or skill areas, and improvements in developmental assets and 21st Century Skills such as critical thinking, communications skills, and problem-solving.

An excellent assessment system for pre-college programs should be longitudinal and should track individual students. The system should have the ability to be integrated with other functions within the university, especially admissions. Postsecondary institutions can use strategic planning activities like logic modeling to articulate program outcomes that are relevant across pre-college programs and to establish benchmarking for outcomes (W. K. Kellogg Foundation, 2004). Individual programs may have needs that a campus-wide approach cannot account for, but a centralized approach will make the most use of limited resources. Developing a data tracking system for pre-college programs requires an investment from institutions, especially in maintaining and updating the system, but improved data systems are necessary for programs to move beyond anecdotal information on program outcomes (Tierney, 2002). With little expertise at the program level and a lack of existing evaluation criteria for college access programs, pre-college programs have a critical need for institutional support for assessment and evaluation (Coles, 1999; Swail & Perna, 2002; Tierney, 2002)—and the investment has the potential to leverage significant benefits for the university and community.

CONCLUSIONS

Pre-college programs serve an important purpose on college campuses and are likely to proliferate as more focus is placed on raising college enrollment and graduation rates. However, accountability pressures and the potential to increase the benefits of pre-college programs for both higher education and the community make it imperative for postsecondary institutions to reevaluate how pre-college programs are supported on campus. Two promising areas for support are the organizational structures around programs and the assessment systems used to measure program outcomes. With limited investment in these two areas, universities can move toward identifying successful programs and elevating pre-college programming as an important function of the engaged university.

About the Author
William Edwards served as a Pre-College Programs Strategist and Assessment Specialist at Michigan State University, during which he authored this article. Following his work at MSU, he served as Director of Institutional Effectiveness for Triton College, Assistant Director of Research and Planning for the City Colleges of Chicago. Since then, he has worked for Sears, Discover Financial Services and now is a Senior Manager of Service Strategy Analytics for Charles Schwab in Colorado.

Originally published as:
Edwards, W. A. (2010, February). Precollege programs and the engaged university. *The Engagement Exchange*, 2. East Lansing: Michigan State University, National Collaborative for the Study of University Engagement.

REFERENCES

Borman, G. D. (2001). Summers are for learning. *Principal, 80*, 26–29.

Calahan, M. W., & Curtin, T. R. (2004, August). *A profile of the Upward Bound program: 2000-2001*. U.S. Department of Education, Office of Postsecondary Education. Retrieved from http://www.ed.gov/programs/trioupbound/ubprofile-00-01.pdf

Choy, S. P., Horn, L. J., Nunez, A.-M., & Chen, X. (2000). Transition to college: What helps at-risk students and students whose parents did not attend college. *New Directions for Institutional Research, 107*, 45-63. Retrieved from http://www3.interscience.wiley.com/journal/101524636/issue

Coles, A. S. (1999). School to college transition programs for low income and minority youth. *Advances in Education Research, 4*, 7-42. Washington, DC: National Library of Education.

Drucker, P. F. (1992). *The age of discontinuity: Guidelines to our changing society*. Piscataway, NJ: Transaction Publishers.

Fairchild, R. A., & Boulay, M. (2002, November). *What if summer learning loss were an education policy priority?* Paper presented at the Association of Public Policy Analysis and Management Conference, Dallas, TX.

Foderaro, L. W. (2009, June 21). For colleges needing cash, summer's no longer a quiet season. *The New York Times*. Retrieved from nytimes.com/2009/06/22/education/22campus.html?_r=1&partner=rss&emc=rss

Haskins, R., Holzer, H., & Lerman, R. (2009, May). *Promoting economic mobility by increasing postsecondary education*. Washington, DC:

Economic Mobility Project. Retrieved from http://www.pewtrusts.org/ our_work_report_detail. aspx?id=51956

Jobs for the Future. (2007, April). *The STEM workforce challenge: The role of the public workforce system in a national solution for a competitive science, technology, engineering, and mathematics (STEM) workforce.* Washington, DC: U.S. Department of Labor. Retrieved from http://www.doleta.gov/Youth_services/pdf/STEM_ Report_4%2007.pdf

Jordan, W. J., & Nettles, S. M. (2000). How students invest their time out of school: Effects on school-related outcomes. *Social Psychology of Education, 3,* 217-243. Retrieved from http://www.springerlink.com/ content/k7h4503635178462

Kane, T. J. (2004, January 16). *The impact of after-school programs: Interpreting the results of four recent evaluations* (Working Paper). New York: W. T. Grant Foundation. Retrieved from http://www.pasesetter.com/ reframe/documents/ThomasKane.pdf

Kellogg Commission on the Future of State and Land-Grant Universities. (1999, February). *Returning to our roots: The engaged institution* (Report No. 3). Washington, DC: National Association of State Universities and Land-Grant Colleges. Retrieved from http://www.aplu.org/ NetCommunity/Page.aspx?pid=305

National Council for Community and Education Partnerships. (2008, August). *Overview of the reauthorization of the Higher Education Act: Gaining Early Awareness and Readiness for Undergraduate Programs (GEAR UP).* Retrieved from www.aau.edu/WorkArea/ DownloadAsset.aspx?id=7336

Pittman, K. J., Irby, M., Yohalem, N., & Wilson-Ahlstrom, A. (2004). Blurring the lines for learning: The role of out-of-school programs as complements to formal learning. *New Directions for Youth Development, 101,* 19-41. Retrieved from http://www3.interscience.wiley.com/ journal/107642320/abstract

Swail, W. S., & Perna, L. W. (2002). Pre-college outreach programs: A national perspective. In W. G. Tierney & L. S. Hagedorn (Eds.), *Increasing access to college: Extending possibilities for all students* (pp. 15-34). Albany, NY: State University of New York Press.

Tierney, W. G. (2002). Reflective evaluation: Improving practice in college preparation programs. In W. G. Tierney & L. S. Hagedorn (Eds.), *Increasing access to college: Extending possibilities for all students* (pp. 217-230). Albany, NY: State University of New York.

U.S. Department of Education. (2008). *21st Century Community Learning Centers: Funding status*. Retrieved from ed.gov/programs/21stcclc/funding.html

U.S. Department of Education, Office of Communications and Outreach. (2008). *Guide to U.S. Department of Education programs*. Washington, DC: Author. Retrieved from http://www.ed.gov/programs/gtep/index.html

U.S. Department of Education, Office of Postsecondary Education. (2006, September). *An interim report of the Talent Search program: 2002-03 and 2003-04, with select data from 2000-02*. Washington, DC: Author. Retrieved from http://www.ed.gov/programs/triotalent/tsinterimreport2002-04.pdf

U.S. Department of Education, Office of Postsecondary Education. (2008a, March). *Upward Bound and Upward Bound Math-Science program outcomes for participants expected to graduate high school in 2004-2005, with supporting data from 2005-2006*. Washington, DC: Author. Retrieved from http://www.ed.gov/about/offices/list/ope/trio/ub-ubms-outcomes-2004.pdf

U.S. Department of Education, Office of Postsecondary Education. (2008b, August). *A profile of the federal TRIO programs and Child Care Access Means Parents in School program*. Washington, DC: Author. Retrieved from http://www.ed.gov/about/offices/list/ope/trio/trioprofile2008.pdf

Vandell, D. L., Reisner, E. R., Brown, B. B., Dadisman, K., Pierce, K. M., Lee, D., & Pechman, E. M. (2005). *The study of promising after-school programs: Examination of intermediate outcomes in year 2* (Report to the Charles Stewart Mott Foundation). Irvine, CA: University of California, Department of Education. Retrieved from http://childcare.gse.uci.edu/pdf/afterschool/reports/PASP%20 Intermediate%20Outcomes.pdf

Venezia, A., & Rainwater, T. (2007). Early outreach. In *State Higher Education Executive Officers (SHEEO), More student success: A systemic solution* (pp. 13-35; DocID 27462). Boulder, CO: SHEEO. Retrieved from http://www.sheeo.org/ pubs/pubs_results.asp?issueID=14

W. K. Kellogg Foundation. (2004, January). *Using logic models to bring together planning, evaluation, and action: Logic model development guide.* Retrieved from http://www.wkkf.org/knowledge-center/ Resources-Page.aspx

Wenger, E., McDermott, R., & Snyder, W. M. (2002). *Cultivating communities of practice: A guide to managing knowledge.* Boston: Harvard Business School Press.

Wiltz, L. K. (2005). I need a bigger suitcase: The evaluator role in non-formal education. *New Directions for Evaluation, 108,* 13-28.

Chapter 3

The History of Organized Pre-College Program Professionals in the United States

By Christopher W. Tremblay, Ed.D.,
Michigan College Access Network

Introduction

Pre-college programming has been documented to date back to 1915 when the University of the Arts launched an office of pre-college programs (Sheth & Tremblay, 2018). Pre-college programming can have a variety of definitions, but for the purposes of this book, we use this one for context:

University sponsored/organized programs and activities for K-12 school participants typically not yet enrolled in college as degree-seeking students.

University departments with responsibility for overall oversight of all pre-college programs at one college or university would be considered a pre-college programming unit, division, office, or department. Pre-college programs like Upward Bound and GEAR UP (Gaining Early Awareness and Readiness for Undergraduate Programs) were launched by the federal government. Upward Bound was formed in 1964 and GEAR UP in 1998. While federally funded, those programs are institutionally located, but may or may not be a part of a pre-college division.

1990s

In 1996, the Association of University Summer Sessions (AUSS) included pre-college programs in its mission, stating, "to provide precollege programs which may serve to recruit students, serve as bridge programs for minority/disadvantaged youth, and/or continuing intellectual development" (n.d., n.p.). This was the first professional association to formally document the inclusion of pre-college programs as part of its mission and serving its members. Historically, most pre-college programming took place in the summer so it made sense that a professional organization focused on summer session would reference and include pre-college programs.

2003-2004

The history of organized pre-college program professionals begins with Bill Holinger (2017), who is affiliated with the Harvard Secondary School Program. At the annual gathering of Pre-College Program Directors in 2017 at the University of Notre Dame, Holinger provided the history in writing about the establishment of the Pre-College Program Directors group. According to Holinger, in Fall 2003, the first such gathering took place at Massachusetts Institute of Technology and included Boston University, Brown University, Cornell University, Columbia College, Duke University, Georgetown University, George Washington University, Harvard University, Ithaca College, Johns Hopkins University, Massachusetts Institute of Technology, Syracuse University, the University of California-Los Angeles, the University of Delaware, Washington University, and Yale University (and a few more). This annual meeting rotated among the member schools, with Columbia College hosting the 2004 meeting. These meetings consisted of telling stories about what happened that past summer. Holinger reflected on the importance of being with his experienced colleagues talking about similar issues and problems. According to him, "We talked about university policy and how it differed from program policy....we talked marketing and admissions; record-keeping and technology; rules & regulations, and discipline..." (p. 1).

2006
In November 2006, a digital listserv emerged as a way to continue those conversations in between the annual meetings. This listserv is currently an invitation-only group in Yahoo! Groups. As of 2017, that listserv had a membership of more than 160 pre-college professionals from across the United States. A Google form has been established to request access to the listserv. *Can I have access?*

2007-2008
Meanwhile, in 2007-2008, planning began for the first Michigan Pre-College and Youth Outreach Conference, which began in Fall 2008 at Michigan State University in East Lansing, Michigan. According to Nick Collins of the University of Michigan, this conference was the idea of and organized by Will Edwards, a graduate student at Michigan State University at the time who was in his doctoral program and interested in youth outreach (personal communication, N. Collins, October 11, 2017). Edwards is the author of Chapter 2. Furthermore, it was in 2008 that the University of Michigan founded the Center for Educational Outreach. That Center was interested in organizing a statewide conference focused on college access and success. The first director of the University of Michigan Center for Educational Outreach, Nick Collins, reached out to Edwards and the University of Michigan hosted the second conference in 2009. Thereafter, participation of the public state universities in Michigan broadened and other schools began hosting the conference, which typically now rotates

throughout the state. That conference continues and celebrated its 10th anniversary in Fall 2017.

2010

In 2010, the North American Association for Summer Schools (NAASS) offered a webinar entitled, "Managing Risk for Pre-College Programs," signaling an interest and involvement in pre-college programming. That was followed by a second webinar on legal aspects in 2011. In 2016, NAASS hosted a pre-conference workshop in Kansas City, Missouri with a focus on scopes, issues, and diversity in the field, presented by Tiffany Oronato and John Robichaux.

2014

Another pre-college related group was forming in 2014. In May 2014, a group of 20 individuals gathered during a regional meeting of the University Risk Management and Insurance Association (URMIA) in Baltimore met to discuss higher education child protection. That association also had accepted a proposal for a youth protection panel at this conference. In 2014, Texas A&M hosted the first "Minors on Campus" conference, which transformed into HEPNet in 2017 (see below). In 2015, Texas A&M University hosted the Minors on Campus Conference. In 2016, that conference was renamed the Conference on Youth Programs in Higher Education.

2015

Similarly, another organization was launching a pre-college event. In Fall 2015, the national Engagement Scholarship Consortium (ESC) created its first pre-college pre-conference workshop in State College, Pennsylvania (on the campus of Pennsylvania State University). ESC continued their pre-college pre-conference workshop with the most recent one in Fall 2019 in Denver, Colorado. The 2017 ESC workshop unveiled a set of 25 pre-college program unit dimensions as guidance for best practices in the field. Those dimensions were created by Susan Sheth and Christopher Tremblay. Also in 2015, Rutgers University presented on K-12 pre-college efforts at the annual ACT Enrollment Planners Conference and did so again in 2016 and 2017.

2017

In May 2017, the Higher Education Protection Network (HEPNet) was officially formed as a national professional association, launching a membership fee, a website, and a members' portal, and continuing their conference in October. HEPNet offered their first webinar to members in September 2017. That webinar was entitled, "A Closer Look at the National Sex Offender Public Website (NSOPW): Benefits and Limitations to Using the Registry to Screen Adults Working with Minors." The 2017 HEPNet conference was held in October on the campus of Clemson University in South Carolina.

In 2017, NAASS formally approached the Pre-College Program Directors group at their fall meeting at the University of Notre Dame with an invitation to affiliate with NAASS. The Pre-College Program Directors decided to maintain independent status and began working to identify ways to meet the needs of the growing numbers of colleagues in the pre-college field.

2018

In 2018, the Pre-College Program Directors group elected their first advisory board to begin formalizing a professional organization.

2019

In 2019, the Advisory Board of the Pre-College Program Directors drafted the first By-Laws of the future "Association for Pre-College Program Directors."

Conclusion

On the national level, there are four separate professional development opportunities for pre-college professionals:

- Engagement Scholarship Consortium Pre-College Conference,
- annual meeting of the Pre-College Program Directors,
- the North American Association of Summer Sessions (NAASS) Pre-College Conference, and
- the annual conference of the Higher Education Protection Network (HEPNet).

Michigan appears to be the only state with a statewide pre-college conference. Currently, all four of these entities are working independently to serve the growing number of professionals in the pre-college field. There is an opportunity to foster collaboration among these organizations to capitalize on their collective voice, create robust professional programming, and streamline efforts. Furthermore, pre-college programs face more scrutiny and visibility. Holinger notes that "things have changed over the years," citing compliance and federal oversight that requires new accountability among pre-college programs.

About the Author

Dr. Christopher W. Tremblay has been active in the pre-college programming space for five years. Tremblay was instrumental in the proposal and establishment of a new Office of Pre-College Programming at Western Michigan

---

University. During his time at the University of Wisconsin-Superior, he had oversight of three TRIO Programs. Tremblay serves as co-editor of the *Journal of College Access*. He has presented at more than 75 association conferences nationally and internationally, including the pre-college workshops at the Engagement Scholarship Consortium's annual conferences. Tremblay served on a special task force within the Pre-College Program Directors group. He currently serves as Director of External Engagement for the Michigan College Access Network (MCAN), where he serves as a member of the Michigan Pre-College and Youth Outreach Conference Steering Committee.

REFERENCES

Association of University Summer Sessions (AUSS) (n.d.). *Mission and Constitution*. Retrieved from http://www.theauss.org/mission-constitution/

Holinger, B. (2017, September 6). Letter documenting the origin and roots of the Pre-College Program Directors.

Sheth, S., & Tremblay, C. (2018, February). *Pre-College Programming Model: 25 Dimensions*. Preliminary Report.

Chapter 4

Starting a Pre-College Program or Office

By Jacqueline T. Newcomb, Ed.D.,
Harvard University

Pre-college programs may be developed for many reasons and may extend a college or university's mission to younger students, increase applications, or generate revenue. The planning process can range from very strategic to basic decision-making requirements such as the type of programming that will be conducted and whether the program will be credit based, non-credit based, or enrichment-only types of classes. Some planning may involve milieu (residential, commuter, online) and the student application and enrollment process (open, selective). This chapter discusses reasons why a university may create a new pre-college program, which decisions need answers, and the campus partners to reach out to for assistance and support services. After considering opportunities and challenges, it concludes with a section on lessons learned.

Starting a Pre-College Program

Many young students are opting to attend courses during the summer more than ever before (Morisi, 2010). This incentivizes college and universities to consider creating various types of pre-college programming. The vision of these programs may vary in length, class-size, subjects, age and grade, and even other audience demographic or socio-economic status. Students choose pre-college programs for numerous reasons such as hoping to get an advantage in the admission process (Jaschik, 2015) while others are obtaining academic skills and determining if college is a realistic possibility for them (Pondiscio, 2013).

Why Establish a Pre-College Program?

There are many reasons why a college or university may establish a new pre-college program. Some pre-college programs try to foster their campus mission of outreach to the community, while others aim to support a particular population of students. Federally-funded TRIO programs such as Upward Bound and Talent Search are designed to encourage high school students from disadvantaged backgrounds to seek opportunities in higher education (U.S. Department of Education, 2014). University and grant funded programs like Summer Bridge (Slade, Eatmon, Staley, & Dixon, 2015) have a similar goal. Some pre-college programs focus on particular academic areas like STEM and increasing academic preparedness and college readiness (Raines, 2012). Summer transition programs have been successful in student retention rates (Simmons, 1994).

Although these programs may not be feeders into their college's admission funnel (Smith-Barrow, 2013), some pre-college programs exist primarily as a recruitment tool and a pipeline for those students. Attending a pre-college program at a less-selective college may give the future admission applicant a leg up not only in preparing them for college but also in gaining admission to that institution. However, there are many other programs that are strictly designed to give students a taste of college life and not advantage them in the admissions process at that university (Carapezza, 2015). These pre-college programs often generate revenue for their campuses (Lundy & Ladd, 2016).

Considerations before Getting Started

When creating any new program, there are a number of key decisions that need to be made, including the establishment of an overall strategy to understand the program's macro and micro needs and reasons as a whole. First, creating a long-term vision plan can assist in evaluating whether the college or university is prepared for minors on campus:

- Where do you want the program to go and by when?
- What barriers might you encounter before, during, or after this program?
- What are the significant concerns?
- What resources do you have to address barriers?
- What needs do you have to meet to overcome barriers? What strategies can you use to address the barriers?
- What strategies can you use to address the overall vision?
- What tools will you create for evaluation?
- How will you show impact?

Once the institution has decided to create and implement a pre-college program, then many micro details need to be addressed. These can include the term(s) offered: summer or academic year (fall, winter, spring), and milieu: residential, commuter, or online. Even these decisions can greatly impact the overall strategy to understand the program needs and reasons as a whole, and the remainder of the planning as services and resources are all tied to these initial questions.

Oftentimes the department where the program will report is already determined. The location of a pre-college program varies greatly from campus to campus. The reporting structure could be within the provost or dean of the college office if they host community outreach or undergraduate admission. On some campuses, pre-college programs are part of continuing education or conference services. Individual academic departments may also conduct their own programs. If there are efforts to consolidate resources, standardize policies and procedures, or mitigate risks of having minors on campus (Carlton, 2015), a university may choose to move all programs under one office or division.

Faculty and Staff
Once the office and structure are known, academic offerings, credit status, instructional and program staff must be determined. Some pre-college programs offer students the opportunity to gain in-depth knowledge of a specific academic discipline such as art and design ("RISD Pre-College," n.d.), while others offer a breadth of courses that mirror the university curriculum ("Harvard Pre-College Program," 2015). The number of days or weeks your program will run may limit the ability to offer credit versus non-credit courses. Shorter programs are often non-credit, as their schedule may not allow enough time to meet the contact hours (Lutes & Davies, 2013) required to give credit to uphold accreditation (Wellman, 2003).

In addition to selecting courses, finding instructors also requires numerous decisions:

- Does university faculty through a course proposal system determine the curriculum?
- Which instructor status is needed to be allowed to teach in the program?
- Can post-docs, university staff, or graduate students teach or only those at the lecturer, assistant, associate, or full professor level?

- Are instructors required to be affiliated with the institution or can external faculty teach?
- How will enrollment limits and course cancelations be determined?

The answers to these questions will need to be resolved before any recruitment efforts can begin. Some universities have faculty workload requirements or restrictions on the number of hours graduate students can work (Kouliavtsev, Kosovich, & Elseth, 2015). In some cases, part-time adjunct faculty may be a viable option (Rhoades, 1996).

New programs might need to hire administrative staff as well as instructors. These staff members may oversee marketing efforts, admission processes, and student affairs functions. Of course, answers about admissions, course registration policies, and finances will be needed before any job descriptions can be finalized:

- Will the program be open enrollment or selective?
- Who will read the applications or process the course registrations?
- Will admission, registrar, and bursar functions be handled internally or by another department on campus?
- Which computer software will be used and will it be integrated with other campus student information systems?
- What will the program cost be for students and will there be financial aid available? Financial aid can help to increase growth in programs (Shin & Sande, 2006).
- How will instructors be compensated?

If publicity will be handled internally, then the person hired should have experience designing websites, advertising, and social media campaigns. Some student affairs functions like residential life and co-curricular event planning could either be managed by the program staff or directly by other campus departments.

Campus Partners
Without campus partners, it would be quite challenging to run a pre-college program. Collaborating with colleagues and other departments will allow students to experience what a typical undergraduate on campus would. Student affairs professionals and the general council staff can assist with risk assessment, the legal language to use on acceptance and waiver forms, policies and any campus protocols for having minors on campus or Title IX compliance. They can also assist in determining any background checks or onboarding requirements for residential staff, teaching assistants, or instructors.

Student Affairs and Campus Services
There are pre-college programs that handle all of their own student affairs functions including housing and co-curricular activities. Others partner with their residential life offices as they would with admissions to provide such services. Additional considerations for services include who will handle crisis management, student discipline, and requests for accessibility accommodations. Will these functions be part of the pre-college office or lie with the professionals who support undergraduates with these matters? Establishing collaborative and positive relationships with faculty, staff members, administrators and other departments will help new programs and staff to establish clout and earn trust (Roueche & Jones, 2010).

Furthermore, specialized services and support may need to come from other departments, such as athletics, ID cards, and dining, library, and health services. New programs should work to determine the extent of services they will offer to their pre-college students:

- Will there be an opportunity for the students to have access to athletic facilities, classes, and intramural sports?
- Will students receive an official university photo ID or a temporary card to use at the dining hall and to enter buildings with swipe card readers?
- Will they receive official university email addresses or other electronic services, or access to download computer software?
- Are instructors offered learning management course sites for their students to use?
- Are pre-college students eligible to use the library as a study space, have borrowing privileges, and view electronic journals and items on reserve?

Computer labs and libraries with access to staff members who provide support are important for pre-college students (Collins, 2009). On many campuses, requests for such services will need to be considered and vetted by a campus-wide committee (Berg, Kraemer, Raatz, & Devoti, 2009) and financial resources may be required to provide services. This is especially important when considering services that the program staff may not have the expertise to deliver, like medical care:

- How will pre-college students receive medical care if needed?
- Will the university health services care for them, will the program staff need to hire their own medical professional(s), or will ill or injured students be transported to a hospital emergency room?

- Will routine medical care be available or only urgent care? How will the program staff support serious mental health concerns?
- Will the pre-college students be able to store and take their own medication or will this be administered by staff?

In any case, the program will need to request medical history and a parent/legal guardian's consent to treat an ill or injured student. Student services will be necessary for pre-college programs with a residential component and academic support may be necessary for any program.

Opportunities

Opportunities for starting a pre-college program can be limitless if the university or college has embraced the idea of having minors on campus and the administration understands the positive effects of implementing these types of programs in higher education settings. Prospective partnerships within the landscape of the institution can bring groups together that may not have had the opportunity to connect and work together before the execution of a pre-college program. Additionally, there are benefits to working with a new student population, such as outreach to the external community through education including supporting various populations and helping to prepare them for college. The program is also a potential new revenue stream for a campus.

If the program takes place during the summer, there may be an opportunity to utilize classrooms, residence and dining halls that may otherwise be empty. The staff that work in these areas and support other campus services may not typically work twelve months, but with a summer program, they may now be able to do so. If the program allows graduate students to serve as course instructors, they will benefit from the teaching experience and supplemental income.

Depending upon the departmental reporting structure and whether the offices are centralized (Buttermore, Baker, & Culp, 2014), a pre-college program could work to develop policies and procedures that are more consistent across campus. At some campuses, programs for minors are housed in various departments including academic disciplines, conference services, athletics, or admission. A standardized reporting structure for programs that serve those younger than traditionally aged undergraduates may better align processes used to manage these students. It is imperative that considerations are made regarding minors on campus in hiring, onboarding including background checks and policies for working with students (Carlton, 2015). The opportunities in creating a new program are numerous, but so are the challenges.

Challenges
With any new program, there will be challenges. Internal challenges can include gaining buy-in from the institution's administration as to the value of a pre-college program. Additionally, these include gaining support of faculty and staff across campus, and ensuring there are staff and financial resources. External challenges may include competition from other programs with similar missions and marketing to recruit potential applicants.

When it comes to getting buy-in from faculty and staff, relationships that build trust are essential (Kezar, 2004). It will be important to reach out to those in departments that may be needed to ensure a successful program and explain the mission and structure of a new program and how they can share in it (Kezar, 2005). Oftentimes, it is the unknown that is more daunting than the time needed for collaboration.

Start-up costs can be another challenge in the development of a new program. When establishing a program, either existing staff members will need to take on this additional work or new staff will need to be hired. If a new staff member is hired, the university will need to fund a position with benefits. An additional consideration is to have an operational budget for the program. Grant funding may be available to help develop and implement a program, especially in the case of unique or underserved populations. Some grants may require data collection so there is a need to consider an institution's capacity to collect this information. A program can also charge tuition or fees to cover program costs and support the sustainability over time.

Another challenge facing new programs is competition for applicants. Understanding what other institutions are offering as well as what other programs exist on campus—such as external competitors coming through conference services—will be important. Successful enrollment managers continually benchmark and stay abreast of what their peer institutions are doing (Humphrey, 2007). Internal and external challenges may seem overwhelming, but with strong strategic planning and supportive collaboration, these challenges can be overcome.

Lessons Learned

There are a number of lessons that this author has learned in her experience starting and running pre-college programs. These include the importance of strategic planning for growth, managing risk, matching the program mission to the campus mission, and assessment. Although strategic planning is a long-term undertaking, enrollment management is typically seen as a short-term endeavor (Gowen & Owen, 1991).

Creating a plan for program growth is essential to a successful program. With any plan, communication is a key component (Lang, 2009). This growth plan should be shared with other stakeholders, including campus offices that support the pre-college instructors and students. Increases in enrollment will impact the number of courses offered, classrooms and residence hall spaces, activities needed, and staffing levels. The program administrators should be willing to take risks and try new options for growth (Roueche & Jones, 2010).

Risk management is crucial for any successful program, especially one that includes under-aged participants. From a comprehensive student handbook to waivers and releases, proactively creating policies and procedures will mitigate risk (Miller & Sorochty, 2014). Even if the program has well established rules, not all risk can be prevented (Kaplan & Mikes, 2012). A good working relationship with colleagues in the general counsel or dean of students office is invaluable. (For more information on risk management, see Chapter 9).

Understanding the purpose of the pre-college program and aligning it with the mission of the institution is vital. When considering the goals or aims of the program, the student admission criteria needs to be included. For example, if the program is housed in a very selective college, then the application decisions should reflect that selectivity. Consulting with the undergraduate office of admission will help program staff to determine criteria as well as minimum English language proficiency needed to be successful. On the other hand, if the pre-college program is geared towards a specific population or part of a less selective institution, keep that in mind when determining enrollment criteria.

Finally, continually assessing and adjusting as needed will lead to a successful program. Students, residential staff, and instructors should be asked to complete program evaluations about their experiences. The program administrators should also review statistical and demographic data about applicants, courses, enrolled students, faculty and staff. Any suggestions for improvement should be considered in future planning. Programs or classes that have high student survey scores may be repeated if possible. Researching new educational trends, other similar pre-college programs and re-aligning annually with the university's goals and mission will help in maintaining a vital program.

There are numerous reasons to create and implement a pre-college program, but a multi-faceted and comprehensive analysis should be conducted before beginning any program. Many questions need to be addressed before any marketing, faculty or course recruitment, or student admission decisions can be made. Hiring, and coordinating student services with other campus departments, are also important pieces of the creation phase. Pre-college programs offer both opportunities and challenges. Using the advice and suggestions from the lessons learned in this chapter can help with the process of starting and executing a pre-college program. Identifying, addressing, and planning for all possibilities is a sensible pro-active approach to a strong quality pre-college program.

About the Author

Jacqueline T. Newcomb started and directs the Harvard Pre-College Program at Harvard University. She earned her Ed.D. from Northeastern University, Ed.M. from the University at Buffalo, and B.A. from the University of Rhode Island. Her dissertation focused on training to detect fraud in international student admissions. She lives in Massachusetts with her husband and two sons.

REFERENCES

Berg, J. E., Kraemer, R., Raatz, C., & Devoti, S. (2009). Building an identity management governance process. *College and University, 84*(3), 20–25.

Buttermore, J., Baker, E., & Culp, D. (2014). Providing affordable access to higher education through year-round operation: A case study in public higher education. *College and University; 89*(4), 2–10, 12–13.

Carapezza, K. (2015, July 24). Wet hot Ivy League summer: Are elite college summer programs worth the price? Retrieved July 28, 2015, from http://blogs.wgbh.org/on-campus/2015/7/24/wet-hot-ivy-league-summer-are-elite-college-summer-programs-worth-price/

Carlton, V. (2015). A need for reform — In the wake of the Penn State scandal: In higher education and K–12 schools. *Brigham Young University Education and Law Journal, 2015*(2). Retrieved from https://digitalcommons.law.byu.edu/cgi/viewcontent.cgi?article=1372&context=elj

Collins, B. L. (2009). Integrating information literacy skills into academic summer programs for precollege students. *Reference Services Review, 37*(2), 143–154.

Gowen, J., & Owen, V. L. (1991). Enrollment management and strategic planning: Resolving a classic tension in higher education. *Nonprofit Management and Leadership, 2*(2), 143–158. doi:10.1002/nml.4130020205

Harvard Pre-College Program. (2015, July 29). Retrieved February 24, 2019, from http://www.summer.harvard.edu/high-school-programs/pre-college-program

Huibregtse, J., Holloway, L. M., & Greenberg, S. (2012). Framingham State University: Faculty and program development. *Continuing Higher Education Review, 76,* 151–158.

Humphrey, K. B. (2007). At the crossroads of access and financial stability: The push and pull on the enrollment manager. *College and University, 82*(1), 11–16.

Jaschik, S. (2015, July 28). Colleges' summer programs don't influence admissions. *Inside Higher Ed.* Retrieved from https://www.insidehighered.com/quicktakes/2015/07/28/colleges-summer-programs-dont-influence-admissions

Kaplan, R. S., & Mikes, A. (2012, June). Managing risks: A new framework. *Harvard Business Review,* 20.

Kezar, A. (2004). What is more important to effective governance: Relationships, trust, and leadership, or structures and formal processes? *New Directions for Higher Education, 2004*(127), 35–46.

Kezar, A. (2005, November 1). Moving from I to we. *Change, 37*(6), 50–57.

Kouliavtsev, M., Kosovich, S., & Elseth, L. (2015). College faculty's labor supply elasticity: Estimates using summer teaching stipends. *Journal of Economics and Economic Education Research, 16*(2), 17–29.

Lang, E. (2009). Sustaining enrollment growth in difficult financial times. *Diverse Issues in Higher Education, 26*(13), 14.

Lundy, K., & Ladd, H. (2016). *Alternative revenues: Can institutions of higher education balance mission and financial goals?* (p. 9). Parthenon-EY Education.

Lutes, L., & Davies, R. (2013). Comparing the rigor of compressed format courses to their regular semester counterparts. *Innovative Higher Education, 38*(1), 19–29. doi:10.1007/s10755-012-9226-z

Miller, T. E., & Sorochty, R. W. (2014). *Risk management in student affairs: Foundations for safety and success.* New York: John Wiley & Sons.

Morisi, T. L. (2010). The early 2000s: A period of declining teen summer employment rates. *Monthly Labor Review, 133*(5), 23.

Pondiscio, R. (2013). "No Excuses" kids go to college. *Education Next*, *13*(2), 8.

Raines, J. (2012). FirstSTEP: A preliminary review of the effects of a summer bridge program on pre-college STEM majors. *Journal of STEM Education: Innovations and Research*, *13*(1), 22–29.

Rhoades, G. (1996). Reorganizing the faculty workforce for flexibility: Part-time professional labor. *The Journal of Higher Education*, *67*(6), 626–659. doi:10.1080/00221546.1996.11774819

RISD Pre-College. (n.d.). Retrieved February 24, 2019, from https://precollege.risd.edu

Roueche, J. E., & Jones, B. R. (2010). Profits in a non-profit world: Celebrating entrepreneurship in the community college. *Community College Journal*, *75*(6), 26–30.

Shin, J.-C., & Sande, M. (2006). Rethinking tuition effects on enrollment in public four-year colleges and universities. *The Review of Higher Education*, *29*(2), 213–237.

Simmons, R. (1994). Precollege programs: A contributing factor to university student retention. *Journal of Developmental Education*, *17*(3), 42–45.

Slade, J., Eatmon, D., Staley, K., & Dixon, K. G. (2015). Getting into the pipeline: Summer Bridge as a pathway to college success. *The Journal of Negro Education*, *84*(2), 125–138.

Smith-Barrow, D. (2013, April 23). Prepare teens for summer college prep programs. *US News & World Report*. Retrieved from https://www.usnews.com/education/high-schools/articles/2013/04/23/prepare-teens-for-summer-college-prep-programs

U.S. Department of Education. (2014). *Federal TRIO Programs 50th anniversary fact sheet*. Retrieved from https://www2.ed.gov/about/offices/list/ope/trio/trio50anniv-factsheet.pdf

Wellman, J. V. (2003). Accreditation and the credit hour. *New Directions for Higher Education*, *2003*(122), 57–69. doi:10.1002/he.110

Chapter 5

25 Dimensions of Pre-College Programming Units in Higher Education

By Christopher W. Tremblay, Ed.D., Michigan College
Access Network & Susan Sheth, Ph.D.,
Michigan State University

Introducing the Dimensions

We developed these 25 dimensions to help represent the standards of a high-quality, pre-college programming unit/office based on our professional experiences and research. Our beta testing results indicated that these dimensions represented a potential tool for assessment of pre-college programming operations and align with recommendations from other researchers. The description for each dimension includes items for consideration.

Page 61 offers a self-assessment tool.

ACCESS AND INCLUSION

Pre-college programming should be accessible to ALL students. Programs and services must not discriminate on the basis of disability; age; race; cultural identity; ethnicity; nationality; family educational history (e.g., first generation to attend college); political affiliation; religious affiliation; sex; sexual orientation; gender identity and expression; marital, social, economic, or veteran status; or any other basis included in institutional policies and codes and laws.

Alternative funding options should be available for low-income students, which may include student scholarships for programming.

COMMUNICATION

Pre-college programming employs a variety of communication tools—website, direct mail, social media, e-mail messages, for example. Communication is targeted to student participants and to parents/families. A directory of all available programming is available and published in print and/or digital formats. If online, directory is searchable by a variety of variables. A calendar of all available programming is available and published in print and/or digital formats. A post-event communication is sent to program participants. This may be done in a print or digital format. Such a follow-up communication should include a survey (unless the survey was conducted as part of the program).

COMPLIANCE

Compliance ensures that all local, institutional, state and federal laws and guidelines are followed, which is paramount to a successful pre-college operation. Works with Risk Management and/or Legal colleagues on campus to ensure such compliance. Develops and annually reviews policies. Maintains a centralized repository of sample forms and documents that can be used by all pre-college programs. Requires all pre-college programs on campus to register with a central office. Policies should include: minors on campus, medical treatment, media releases, parent/guardian consent forms, rights/responsibilities, transgender protocol, and the Children's Online Privacy Protection Act (COPPA). Policies should be published publicly and shared with participants and families for optimal transparency.

COMPREHENSIVE

Pre-college programming must be inclusive of all programming offered to K-12 students. Inclusivity means academic and non-academic entities (including athletics). All programming includes federally funded programming (Upward Bound, GEAR UP), summer programming (camps), sports camps, college access programs, gifted/talented programs, and high school dual enrollment. Programming may or may not take place on a college campus, but should be organized or hosted by the college/university.

EMERGENCY PREPAREDNESS

Emergency procedures are documented and published. Emergency procedures are included in required training of all staff. Scenarios/table top exercises are performed to test the emergency procedures. Emergency alert systems are made available to pre-college programming participants. Emergency procedures are shared with an Office of Risk Management. *Safety Scott?*

EVALUATION AND ASSESSMENT

Regular evaluation and assessment of all initiatives to determine effectiveness is conducted. On-going evaluation and assessment should include survey of student participants. Periodically uses an external evaluator to gain additional perspective. Evaluation and assessment results are used to implement improvements in future programming. An assessment plan exists. Uses data sources (i.e., National Student Clearinghouse) to track students from pre-college through college graduation.

EXTERNAL RELATIONS

Establishes partnerships off-campus. Some programming is offered in conjunction with community organizations. Knows the community. Plays a role in identifying community needs.

Assists with meeting the needs of the community. Is active in community organizations. Participates in community asset mapping if requested.

FOSTERS LIFELONG LEARNING

Pre-college programming inspires participants to learn for the rest of their lives. Programming should plant the seed for students to understand the importance of learning every day. Promotes the pursuit of graduate and/or professional school. Presents and represents all postsecondary educational options to students/families.

INNOVATION

Pre-college programming is cutting-edge and constantly evolving to meet the needs and demands of students K-12. Programming integrates creativity into the learning process, where possible. *How can we innovate & try new things?*

INTEGRATED

Pre-college programming should be integrated for the purposes of sharing resources, optimizing the calendar, maximizing exposure. Such integration allows for coordination among programs to complement each other and generate synergies. *What does integration mean here?*

LEADERSHIP

All impt aspects of leader' role

A pre-college programming unit must have a leader designated to establish a vision, make decisions, establish policies and procedures, write a strategic plan, and supervise a team and all programming using all resources available. Has sufficient staffing resources to execute the goals and mission. Has full support from senior administration on campus (for the encouragement of high level of engagement with central unit and for the enforcement of policies).

LINKED TO MISSION

Pre-college programming should be aligned with the mission of the organization. Colleges/universities should do a review of each program to determine how each program aligns with the mission.

engages students within a community of learners committed to building a ~~more~~ just & compassionate world

OUTCOMES-DRIVEN

Pre-college programming should have outcomes that are measured. Outcomes should be aligned with mission and should consider all aspects of outreach, engagement, learning, and institutional benefits (financial, enrollment, etc.). Specifically stated learning outcomes should be documented, communicated, and evaluated to ensure outcomes are being met. Student learning outcomes should be listed on a pre-college programming webpage.

PLANNING

Pre-college programming includes a written strategic plan and annual action plans. The strategic plan should be for two to five years. The strategic plan aligns with the University's strategic plan, where possible. Annual action plans include new efforts/improvements, and specific goals for that year. Action plans align with the strategic plan. The entire team in the unit is involved with planning.

PREPARATION FOR POSTSECONDARY OPTIONS

Programming offers resources (presentations, print/digital materials, information) about how to prepare for postsecondary options, including enrollment in college. *can be doing more of this*

PRE-RECRUITMENT

Pre-college programming includes some pre-recruitment elements such as: admissions presentation, recruitment literature, etc. Names of pre-college program participants are shared with the admissions office so students can be added to the customer relationship management (CRM) in order to receive information about upcoming admissions-related events like open houses. Student participants can "opt out" of such communication and such an option should be provided on the program registration page.

PROGRAM RATIONALE
Each pre-college program articulates audience(s) served and need(s) being met. Programs should not be solely based on the author's/creator's personal interests.

PROGRAM SUSTAINABILITY
Pre-college programming is built with a foundation that will last for a number of years (unless attendance is low). Programming does not rely solely on one person's vision/effort. Succession planning for program coordination and instruction is considered.

RECOGNIZED DIVISION
Pre-college programming—when more than three such initiatives exist on a college campus—should be organized under one umbrella structure for efficiency and effectiveness. This can be as a department, center, or division, for example.

REPORTING
Pre-college programming annually reports progress, programs offered, and demographics on students served and goals met. Reports are shared with college administrators and published in an accessible portion of a department's website for public transparency. Reports are also shared with all individuals/organizations on campus involved in pre-college programming. Each separate program/activity is required to submit an annual report (even if only a short one-pager).

RESEARCH, PUBLISHING, AND PRESENTING

Pre-college programming staff regularly researches emerging trends in the field, strives to become an expert in the field of pre-college programming. Pre-college leaders publish results and best practices, study effective programs at other places, and present at conferences.

RESOURCED

HUMAN RESOURCES:

Enough part-time, temporary, and full-time staff to accomplish the goals and fulfill the mission.

FINANCIAL RESOURCES:

A budget large enough to implement programming. This may also include a funding plan to generate new revenue. Applies for local, state, institutional, federal, and foundational grants to support programming. Sponsorships of programming should be considered. Has an account set up with the Development Office to receive donations and promotes that opportunity on the pre-college programs website. Writes grants for external funding support.

TECHNOLOGICAL RESOURCES:

Technical tools like a CRM, registration systems, computers, etc., should be available to support the programming offered.

STUDENT DEVELOPMENT

Pre-college programming has elements of enhancing a student's learning and development. Programming should be aligned with or based on the major student development theories. → what are these?

STUDENT ENGAGEMENT

Pre-college programming is interactive and engaging of participants. Pre-college programming places the student participant at the center and avoids lecture-style as much as possible. Programming reflects the latest instructional strategies based on recent developments in the field of education. Experiential programming is highly recommended.

TRAINING

Provides regular, on-going, in-person training to faculty and staff. Topics should include compliance, best practices, university protocol, and all of the dimensions covered in this tool. Training for establishers of new programs is required before programs are launched.

Using the Dimensions for Self-Assessment

RATING SCALE

We have created a rating scale that can be used with each Dimension:

4 = Exemplary
3 = Exceeds
2 = Meets
1 = Partly Meets
0 = Does Not Meet

Scale was adapted with permission from the Council for the Advancement of Standards (cas.edu)

Use the chart on the next page to complete a self-assessment. Total scores will range from 0 (non-existent) to 100 (standard of excellence).

Self-Assessment

DIMENSION	SELF SCORE (1 to 5)
Access and Inclusion	
Communication	
Compliance	
Comprehensiveness	
Emergency Preparedness	
Evaluation and Assessment	
External Relations	
Fosters Lifelong Learning	
Innovation	
Integrated	
Leadership	
Linked to Mission	
Outcomes Driven	
Planning	
Preparation for Postsecondary Options	
Pre-Recruitment	
Program Rationale	
Program Sustainability	
Recognized Division	
Reporting	
Research, Publishing, and Presenting	
Resourced	
Student Development	
Student Engagement	
Training	
TOTAL	

The continuum in Table 1 on the next page shows the five stages that a pre-college program department/office may be in.

Table 1. Continuum and Stages.

Pre-College Programs Organizational Continuum and Stages

Non-Existent	Emerging	Established	Developing	Standard of Excellence
No Pre-College Programs	Some Pre-College Programs But No Separate Office	Division/Unit/Office of Pre-College Programs	Meets Some of the 25 Dimensions	Meets All 25 Dimensions of Model

About the Authors

Dr. Susan Sheth is the director of Gifted and Talented Education at MSU. Prior to her time at MSU, Susan taught communications at the University of Michigan for 12 years before pursuing gifted education. Her pursuits for the gifted include creating more opportunities, building stronger educational curricula, and identification of gifted students. Susan received her Ph.D. from the University of Toledo in Curriculum and Instruction of Gifted Education. Sheth is currently the president of the Michigan Association for Gifted Children and is Northwestern University's Midwest Academic Talent Search Program liaison for southeast and mid-Michigan.

Dr. Christopher W. Tremblay has been active in the pre-college programming space for five years. Tremblay was instrumental in the proposal and establishment of a new Office of Pre-College Programming at Western Michigan University. During his time at the University of Wisconsin-Superior, he had oversight of three TRIO Programs. Tremblay serves as co-editor of the *Journal of College Access*. He has presented at more than 75 association conferences nationally and internationally, including the pre-college workshops at the Engagement Scholarship Consortium's annual conferences. Tremblay served on a special task force within the Pre-College Program Directors group. He currently serves as Director of External Engagement for the Michigan College Access Network (MCAN), where he serves as a member of the Michigan Pre-College and Youth Outreach Conference Steering Committee.

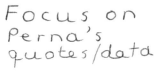
Chapter 6

Pre-College Programs Designed to Increase Access to Higher Education

By Kim Lijana, Ph.D., University of Michigan

Pre-college programs or college access programs exist because students enroll in college at different rates based on their demographic background and experiences. In the United States, there is a persistent post-secondary enrollment rate gap based on family income. According to the National Center for Education Statistics (2017), the immediate college enrollment rate[1] between 1972 and 1980 was approximately 50 percent. The rate increased to 67 percent by the late 1990s, dropping in the early 2000s to 62 percent before increasing again to 67 percent, where it remains today. Despite an overall narrowing of the college enrollment gap, the immediate college enrollment rates of high school completers from low- and middle-income families trailed those of their peers from high-income families by more than 10 percentage points over the last four decades. In 2014, the immediate college enrollment rate for high school completers from low-income families was 52 percent, while the rate for middle-income families was 64 percent and high-income families was 81 percent. In addition to enrollment gaps based on income, there are consistent gaps based on gender and race/ethnicity. A higher percentage of women enroll than men. Students who are Asian are most likely to

---

[1] The immediate college enrollment rate is defined as the percentage of high school completers of a given year who enroll in two- or four-year colleges in the fall immediately after completing high school.

enroll followed by White, Hispanic, and Black students. From the early 2000s to 2017, the enrollment rate increased for Asian students (87 percent from 74 percent), Hispanic students (67 percent from 49 percent), and White students (69 percent from 65 percent), while remaining unchanged for Black students (58 percent).

Pre-college programs focused on access to higher education typically target students who are under-represented in higher education, which includes low-income students, students of color, first generation, and geographically diverse students. The intention of these programs is to provide under-represented students with the skills, knowledge, and general college preparation required to enter and succeed in college (Perna & Swail, 2001). Unfortunately, there is a significant gap between what public K-12 education in the United States prepares all students for and the requisite expectations for college and university success; a particular emphasis is often placed on the steps necessary to apply and enroll in postsecondary education because the process is so complex, especially for students who are unfamiliar with the steps and under-represented in higher education. Pre-college programs attempt to fill in the gap, and evidence suggests that pre-college programs can increase access for under-represented students (Perna, 2002).

College access programs (CAP) implement interventions and strategies to increase the likelihood that children of low-income families will be ready to apply to, enroll in, and succeed in postsecondary institutions at rates comparable to those of their more affluent peers. The first CAPs started in churches, and in the late 1960s three federal CAPs emerged titled "TRIO": Upward Bound, Talent Search, and Student Support Services (Gullatt & Jan, 2003). These programs were designed to increase student access to postsecondary education for students who were historically underrepresented in higher education. Upward Bound profoundly influenced CAPs that were established after its introduction (Gullatt & Jan, 2003). Upward Bound and programs modeled off it were focused on providing individual students with opportunities. However, a new trend emerged during President Clinton's second term—instead of focusing on providing opportunities for individual students, collaborations were formed through partnerships to serve entire schools (Gullatt & Jan, 2003). GEAR UP is a federally funded college access program that exists among a number of private, not-for-profit, state-, and federal-level agencies, all providing college preparation and outreach (U.S. Department of Education, 2019). Similar to the influence Upward Bound had on the programs designed after it, GEAR UP has inspired a new type and style of CAP that focuses on a school-wide intervention.

Cultural and social capital development is one theoretical underpinning for the many pre-college initiatives that seek to have a positive influence on college access. CAPs designed for students of lower socioeconomic status (SES) aim to provide students with a network of services with associated benefits to increase low-income students' access to valued social and cultural capital. Building a network that facilitates school success and leads to college enrollment provides a means for students to develop college aspirations while accessing important information and guidance on how to prepare for college academically, socially, and financially.

CAPs typically have the same intended outcomes: college enrollment and college success. However, the services offered with the logic that college enrollment will result vary. Outreach services based on program component are outlined in Table 1. Programs serve students starting as early as middle school to and even at times through college.

Table 1. Outreach services by program component.

Program Component	Typical services provided	Example
College Counseling/ Awareness: Disseminates information; provides advising and counseling	Advising and counseling, application assistance, workshops, campus visits, test preparation classes	College Advising Corps: High school-based program that helps students identify, apply for, and select a college and secure financial assistance.
Academic Support: Prepares students to take and succeed in college-level course work	Academic courses, test preparation, summer programs, academic advising, tutoring, workshops	Upward Bound: Provides after-school and summer instruction to low-income high school students on a college campus.
Personal and Social Enrichment: Helps students to build confidence, motivation, and awareness of strengths and weaknesses	Leadership, social and professional development seminars, field trips, peer groups, cultural activities	Gifted Student Programming: Provides enriching academic experiences and increases critical thinking, creativity and self-esteem.
Parental Involvement: Assists parents with learning about college and supporting students' goals and activities	Orientation activities, volunteer opportunities, awareness programs, and workshops for parents	Transitions Workshop: A summer program for parents of high school sophomores and juniors to learn about financial aid and job market trends.
Mentoring: Provides one-on-one personalized guidance and role models	Mentoring, tutoring, workshops, cultural programming, field trips, peer learning groups	I Have A Dream (IHAD): Long-term program of mentoring, tutoring and enrichment for low-income students.
Career-Based Outreach: Links academic preparation to college majors, career goals, and long-term career planning	College preparatory courses, career planning and counseling, tutoring, field trips	STEM Programs: Provide exposure to specific disciplines, offer hands-on experiences.

Program Component	Typical services provided	Example
Financial Assistance: Provides college scholarships and/or helps students apply for and secure money for college	Advising and counseling, workshops, scholarship application assistance, and scholarships and grants.	Gates Millennium Scholarship 21st Century Scholars Achievers Scholarship

This is just one way to organize programs. Other options would be by program location, program funding, or target participants (i.e., schools or individuals).

Research on College Outreach Programs

In a quantitative study, Perna (2002) examined 1,100 college outreach programs to determine if they included the key elements identified through research that support students through Hossler and Gallagher's (1987) three-stage college choice framework. In her study, Perna identified five critical program components that support students through the stages and predict college enrollment: a goal of college attendance; college tours, visits, or fairs; a goal of rigorous course taking; a parent component; and that the program begins by grade eight (Perna, 2002). Only 25 percent of the programs targeting students historically underrepresented in higher education (low-income, first-generation, students of color) included at least the five critical components that predict college enrollment.

Using data from the 1988 National Education Longitudinal Study (NELS:88), NCES has defined the key elements in the pipeline to college as: aspirations, academic preparation, college entrance exams (SAT/ACT), college admissions application, and enrollment. A balanced access model has been created, which infuses financial access into the NCES Model (St. John, Musoba, Simmons, Chung, Schmit & Peng, 2004). In the balanced access model, perceived unmet financial need is added to family income and family background, indicating that financial factors influence student aspirations and student plans. Actual unmet financial need is added to expose its impact on college admissions applications and college choice.

Even though the critical elements have been identified, the lack of rigorous evaluation—and in some cases any evaluation—seriously limits our understanding of outreach programs' effectiveness. Gándara and Bial (2001) reviewed 33 college access programs; they concluded that the absence of longitudinal data on the students, limited evidence of academic achievement, and student attrition all limited our understanding of college outreach programs.

Evaluations have been conducted on the government college access programs, like Upward Bound, GEAR UP, and Talent Search. Unfortunately, a significant amount of the evaluation work has shown inconsistent or disappointing results or little to no effect on the following outcomes: high school graduation, four-year college enrollment, GPA, and high school course selection (ACT, 2007; Constantine, Seftor, Martin, Silva & Myers, 2006; Myers, Olsen, Seftor, Young & Tuttle, 2004). Myers et al.'s (2004) experimental evaluation of Upward Bound and Constantine et al.'s (2006) quasi-experimental evaluation of Talent Search both found positive effects for the following: students with low initial educational expectations, financial aid application, and in-state college enrollment. A more recent quasi-experimental design using Educational Longitudinal Study (ELS) data found that targeted outreach programs do little to change educational experiences of their participants (Domina, 2009). Building on the Domina (2009) findings, Glennie, Dalton, and Knapp (2015) used ELS data and found that precollege access programs influence the likelihood that participants will acquire information about college opportunities, as well as, financial aid offered to students. Despite that, using a comparison group they did not find a difference in terms of enrollment in college and found that pre-college program participants persisted at a lower rate into their second year of college than non-participants.

In comparison to the other college access programs, the programs that have been studied the most are foundation funded financial aid programs including the Gates Millennium Scholars program, the Washington State Achievers, and the federally-funded TRIO and GEAR UP programs just discussed. Program evaluation was built into the program design; the Gates Millennium Scholars was established in 1999 with a $1 billion investment into a 20-year project. The federal investment into two of the available college access programs, Upward Bound and GEAR UP, annually is more than half a billion dollars. When the federal government and private foundations make significant investments into programs, they rely on evaluations to determine if the program works and if the investment is worthwhile. Typically, higher education pre-college programs and community-based programs are investing most of their resources into direct support and have limited resources and technical expertise invested in research and evaluation efforts.

DesJardins and McCall (2006) used a regression-discontinuity design to examine the effects of participating in the Gates Millennium Scholars program. They found causal evidence that the program causes lower loan debt, higher retention, and reduced work hours for the low-income, high ability, minority students served by the program. Since the primary component of the program is a significant scholarship, the findings are aligned with the program design. Data limitations prevented the researchers from estimating the effects on college completion and other important outcomes related to career acquisition and application to additional education beyond the baccalaureate.

Overall, the findings of rigorous research studies examining college access programs have been mixed at best. Thus far, it has not discouraged investment in these programs or altered the program goals of encouraging students to pursue and complete higher education. Studying pre-college programs is complex for a few important reasons. As highlighted in Table 1 on pages 68-69, pre-college programs have multiple components and strategies. The large-scale randomized control trials (the gold standard of education research) study multiple programs together using control groups. This limits our understanding of individual programs or the qualities of the program that may be most important. The most recent evaluation highlights the importance of programs focusing on the long-term preparation that will support students in staying enrolled at a postsecondary institution. To evaluate program effectiveness requires building postsecondary longitudinal data systems that track students from these programs. More is known about the federal pre-college programs than higher education and community based college access and pre-college programming.

**Pre-College Access Programs:
Higher Education Institutions**
In addition to the school-wide outreach initiatives, higher education institutions run a complement of programs to increase college access and postsecondary aspirations. The goal of these programs is to increase college enrollment and success broadly and at times at their specific institution. Using publicly available information from the university websites, three innovative university-based pre-college programs are highlighted: University of Michigan's Wolverine Pathways program, Rutgers University's Future Scholars program, and University of Chicago's Collegiate Scholars program.

University of Michigan Wolverine Pathways

Wolverine Pathways is a free, year-round selective admissions college readiness program for seventh to twelfth grade students who live in three geographic areas in Michigan: Ypsilanti, Southfield, or Detroit. The goal of the program is to prepare students for selective college admission by supporting students in their academic and social development. Programming occurs on the weekends and during the summer and focuses on community involvement, leadership, and academic performance, including a focus on essay writing and college admission exam success. Students who complete the program and are admitted into the University of Michigan-Ann Arbor or University of Michigan-Dearborn receive a four-year tuition scholarship. The program leverages the vast resources at the University of Michigan for meaningful on-campus experiences, college preparation workshops, exposure to various disciplines and career pathways, as well as experiences interacting and being mentored by University of Michigan undergraduate students, faculty, and staff. You can learn more about the program here: wolverinepathways.umich.edu

Rutgers University Future Scholars

The goal of the Rutgers Future Scholars program is to increase the number of promising students who complete high school, encourage them to apply to attend post-secondary institutions including Rutgers University, and develop a replicable model to incite peer institutions in-state and nationwide. Rutgers Future Scholars annually accepts 200 first-generation, low-income, academically promising middle school students from five communities in New Jersey: New Brunswick, Piscataway, Newark, Camden, and Rahway. Each site serves 250 scholars and starting the summer before eighth grade, students participate in university programming and events and begin receiving support and mentoring that continues throughout their high school and college years. The program is intended to supplement their school experiences with honors classes, cultural events, career skills, sports, and more to prepare students for college by offering hope, opportunity and a full tuition scholarship for students who successfully complete the five-year program. Annual summer programming takes place at the Rutgers campus located in their community. All scholars are required to attend mentoring, college readiness, enrichment, academic support, and team building seminars that occur throughout the summer and during the school year through a seminar series and monthly cohort meetings. You can learn more about the program here: futurescholars.rutgers.edu

University of Chicago Collegiate Scholars

The University of Chicago Collegiate Scholars program is designed to encourage high achieving and underrepresented Chicago Public Schools students to apply to and succeed at highly selective colleges and universities. The program is shaped around a core curriculum of humanities, social science, math, and science courses that are taught during the summer by University of Chicago faculty and Ph.D. candidates. Enrichment activities during the academic year are geared toward college readiness, leadership development, civic engagement, and cultural exploration. University of Chicago Collegiate Scholars accepts a diverse group of exceptional ninth grade Chicago Public School students to participate in a three-year college readiness program. Program participants participate annually in a six-week summer program. During the school year, scholars participate in two college advising sessions and choose at least 10 events per year focused on leadership development, college readiness, and more on the weekends and evenings. Students participate in campus visits locally and nationally, complete test prep courses, and attend college preparatory workshops along with year-round college admissions mentorship. The goal of the program is that students have the greatest number of options available when selecting colleges and better understand what to consider when making this important decision. You can learn more about the program here: collegiatescholars.uchicago.edu/

Program Elements
You may have noticed that all the programs start early, reaching students in middle school or at the beginning of their high school career. These three programs offer three different approaches to student selection. All the programs require applications, but U-M's program focuses on accepting middle school students from three geographic regions without an emphasis on school attended: Rutgers' program annually accepts 200 first-generation, low-income, academically promising middle school students from five New Jersey communities; University of Chicago's Collegiate Scholars program serves ninth graders from one district, Chicago Public Schools. All the programs focus on academic preparation to complement what students are learning in their school experience, as well as an array of college readiness practices to support development of student aspirations and the college application process. In addition, University of Michigan and Rutgers University are providing a full tuition scholarship to address student and family financial concerns and constraints. Going back to the research, these programs include most if not all the components that increase the likelihood students will enroll and succeed in higher education. These institutions are making substantial investments early in students to benefit their institution, their state, and the country.

About the Author

Kim Lijana is Director of the University of Michigan's Center for Educational Outreach. She received her Ph.D. from U-M's Center for the Study of Higher and Postsecondary Education and co-authored two books, *Left Behind: Urban High Schools and the Failure of Market Reform* (2015) and *Using Action Inquiry in Engaged Research: An Organizing Guide* (2017). Kim is passionate about providing life-changing opportunities for students and has developed a strong track record for increasing postsecondary education access and success for low-income, first-generation, and underrepresented students.

REFERENCES

ACT. (2007). *Using EXPLORE and PLAN data to evaluate GEAR UP programs.* Washington, DC: National Council for Community and Education Partnerships.

Constantine, J. M., Seftor, N., Martin, E. S., Silva, T., & Myers, D. (2006). *A study on the effect of the Talent Search program on secondary and post-secondary outcomes in Florida, Indiana, and Texas.* Washington, DC: U.S. Department of Education, Office of Planning, Evaluation, and Policy Development.

DesJardins, S. L., & McCall, B. P. (2006). *The impact of the Gates Millennium Scholars Program on the college enrollment, borrowing and work behavior of low-income minority students.* Report to the Bill and Melinda Gates Foundation.

Domina, T. (2009). What works in college outreach: Assessing targeted and schoolwide interventions for disadvantaged students. *Educational Evaluation and Policy Analysis, 31*(2), 127–152.

Gándara, P., & Bial, D. (2001). *Paving the way to postsecondary education: K–12 intervention programs for underrepresented youth.* Washington, DC: U.S. Department of Education, National Center for Educational Statistics, Office of Educational Research and Improvement.

Glennie, E., Dalton, B., & Knapp, L. (2015). The influence of precollege access programs on postsecondary enrollment and persistence. *Educational Policy, 29*(7), 963–983.

Gullatt, Y., & Jan, W. (2003). *How do pre-collegiate academic outreach programs impact college-going among underrepresented students?* Retrieved from http://citeseerx.ist.psu.edu/viewdoc/ download?doi=10.1.1.483.7094&rep=rep1&type=pdf

Hossler, D., & Gallagher, K. S. (1987). Studying student college choice: A three phrase model and the implications for policymakers. *College and University, 2*(3), 207–221.

Myers, D., Olsen, R., Seftor, N., Young, J., & Tuttle, C. (2004). *The impacts of regular Upward Bound: Results from the third follow-up data collection.* Washington, DC: Mathematic Policy Research.

National Center for Educational Statistics. (2017). *Immediate college enrollment rate.* Retrieved June 20, 2019, from https://nces.ed.gov/ programs/coe/indicator_cpa.asp

Perna, L. W. (2002). Precollege outreach programs: Characteristics of programs serving historically underrepresented groups of students. *Journal of College Student Development, 43*(1), 64–83.

Perna, L., & Swail, W. (2001). Pre-college outreach and early intervention. *Thought & Action, 17*(1), 99–110.

Rutgers University Future Scholars. (2019). Retrieved June 20, 2019 from futurescholars.rutgers.edu/app/content/aboutUs.jsp

St. John, E. P., Musoba, G. D., Simmons, A., Chung, C.-G., Schmit, J., & Peng, C.-Y. J. (2004). Meeting the access challenge: An examination of Indiana's Twenty-first Century Scholars Program. *Research in Higher Education 45*(8), 829–871.

United States Department of Education. (2019). *Gaining Early Awareness and Readiness for Undergraduate Programs (GEAR UP).* Retrieved June 20, 2019 from https://www2.ed.gov/programs/gearup/index.html

University of Chicago Collegiate Scholars. (2019). Retrieved June 20, 2019 from collegiatescholars.uchicago.edu/

University of Michigan Wolverine Pathways. (2019). Retrieved June 20, 2019 from wolverinepathways.umich.edu/about-the-program/

Chapter 7

Pre-College Programming as Enrollment

By Meghan Groome, Ph.D. and Kacey McCaffrey,
The School of the New York Times

Pre-College Programs and Institutional Goals
*Talent Pipeline and Investing in Students Prior to
Undergraduate Enrollment*

The pipeline is a term borrowed from the human capital model of economic development. It posits that human talent and capacity is a major input regarding economic development and must be considered when conducting long-range planning. The talent pipeline is a clumsy but useful metaphor—individuals enter the pipeline or pathway when they enter an education system and continue along through their work career. For a region to grow economically, policymakers must think about what skills, attributes, and capacity individuals must have to participate in the economy and build their education system to produce those types of people. It is a way of thinking often at odds with educators as it reduces students to passengers in the education system, but it builds both a compelling case for long-term investment in individuals and serves as a useful planning model for educators (Thomasian, 2011).

Higher education is shifting, and the top performing colleges are becoming more competitive while others struggle to stay open. This chapter examines how the talent pipeline builds a compelling case for investment in pre-college programs and how it can be used to plan for students to move along the pathway from pre-college applicant to active alumni. Shifting admissions patterns mean that colleges must do a better job of finding the right candidates (Belkin, 2019). As more students use pre-college programs to experience a "taste" of campus life, colleges can deploy pre-college programs to build a pipeline of talented students who are a good fit for the campus.

The Case for Pre-College Programs
Institutions consider adding pre-college programs to their campus for various reasons, ranging from revenue generation to increased academic success for incoming students. While there are numerous benefits to adding pre-college programs, they also bring different challenges to a college than other populations. For the most part, pre-college programs work with a population who is under 18 years old and must be managed under additional legal and regulatory frameworks (see Chapter 9). These challenges often make campus leadership hesitant to host pre-college programs. For those risks to be worthwhile, and to make the case for pre-college programs, institutions should question how pre-college programs advance the mission of the college and benefit the institution. An institution should ask itself a few key questions to help guide program design:

- How does a pre-college program support your mission?
- What other self-serving benefits may come from pre-college programs?
- How can you align pre-college programs with campus enrollment needs?

The answers to these questions can help managers build a compelling case for pre-college programs as well as identify stakeholders and their priorities. It is essential that pre-college program managers develop strong relationships across academic, student life, and operational units within the institution to determine institutional priorities. Pre-college programs can confer a myriad of direct benefits to the campus community, from new sources of revenue to improved town-gown relationships. The remainder of this section reviews some of the possible benefits of pre-college programs.

Revenue generation. As institutions feel the pressure to limit or reduce rising tuition costs on students, the need for creative and additional revenue sources has increased (Marcus, 2017). Pre-college programs may offer a new source of revenue in the form of program tuition and out-side grants. In addition, many pre-college programs happen during the summer and subsidize operations that otherwise may not be able to operate year-round. One of the prime examples include housing/dining operations that can benefit from filling empty beds and dining halls during the summer months.

Local community building. While many programs offer residential programs that bring in non-local students, many also offer non-residential or day programs that can be designed to maximize interactions with local schools and students. Creating opportunities for local students can improve town-gown relationships. This improved relationship can also create pathways between local high schools and the institution, thus possibly increasing the likelihood of applications from local students. The International Town & Gown Association provides numerous resources on community building for institutions that can be applied to pre-college programs.

Campus enrollment needs. The second half of this chapter will examine the application of the enrollment funnel in regard to pre-college programs, but the larger questions are:

- How can a pre-college program support campus enrollment needs?
- Is the campus struggling to attract students in the STEM fields? International students? Local or non-local students?

By articulating the enrollment needs of the campus, pre-college program designers can build programs that identify and introduce key groups of students to the campus and under-enrolled departments.

Retention efforts. As higher education scholars continue to build on the work of Tinto (2006) as well as Kinzie and Kuh (2004), institutions are investing time and resources in retention efforts. As Kramer (2007) suggests, transition programs, such as pre-college programs, can be a strategy to improve retention rates. Pre-college students who study on a particular campus may get an immersive introduction to that campus which could create an affinity between the student and the campus. That connection can foster a stronger connection between the institution and the student before they even begin their undergraduate career.

Academic success. While many pre-college programs cannot offer transferable college credit, they can ensure that they provide a rigorous academic experience that will help prepare students for college coursework. The importance and meaning of academic rigor is continually debated. However, scholars have widely accepted Nordvall and Braxton's (1996) definition of academic rigor as "the level of understanding of course content to be demonstrated by students while engaging in course-level processes" and that the highest level of understanding can be assessed by asking students to evaluate course content versus content recall, the lowest indicator of comprehension (p. 486). The academic rigor offered by pre-college programs can assist in preparing students for academic success in their undergraduate studies.

In addition to the benefits listed above, there are other, sometimes intrinsic, benefits of pre-college programs. As mentioned before, it is imperative that pre-college managers identify their institution's priorities when proposing a new pre-college program. Sometimes the true goals and needs of an institution are only known by a few key stakeholders. One of the many challenges that pre-college program managers will face is identifying decision makers and key stakeholders who will lead to answers to the questions listed earlier, which in turn will form stronger cases for pre-college programs.

Pre-College Candidates—Marketing and Enrollment
The first half of the chapter borrowed the concept of a pipeline from economic development and focused on how pre-college programs can impact an institution. The second half is guided by concepts found in the marketing world and focused on the recruitment of pre-college students. In order to better examine how prospects can move from the applicant to the current student stage, pre-college program managers should be familiar with the marketing funnel. Perna (2005) took the concept of the marketing funnel and translated it for education to the enrollment funnel. Pre-college managers can adapt this funnel to describe the process of developing loyalty with students and their families, transferring the relationship from marketing lead to pre-college participant to undergraduate student.

Marketing 101: Importance of a formal marketing plan

Pre-college programs can pull from the marketing plans of their institution, but must ultimately create a separate plan inclusive of those resources as well as a plan to reach their target audience. As such, pre-college program managers should be familiar with the marketing style of the greater institution but also the unique qualities of their program. Pre-college programs must also be cognizant of laws regarding advertising to minors and/or their parents including the Child Online Protection Act (COPA). Marketing plans should include plans for both digital (e.g., Google Ads, social media, etc.) and content (e.g., blogs, newsletters, etc.).

Creating a persona. Determining your ideal pre-college candidate can be challenging without a model or framework. The marketing concept of a persona can be applied to pre-college admissions/marketing and program design. While there are whole courses in how marketers generate a persona, the Digital Communications Division in the U.S. Department of Health and Human Services' (HHS) Office also offers public resources regarding personas. Marketers create a persona that is a composite of an ideal candidate. Pre-college program managers can pull from this theory by using quantitative and qualitative research to create ideal candidate profiles for each pre-college program based on their program's attributes. When creating personas, managers should also consider personas for student guardians and other influencers on a student's decision to apply and ultimately enroll in a pre-college program. Based on suggestions of Hisanabe (2009), pre-college managers can utilize personas to visualize and understand the unique needs of stakeholders. Keeping their personas in mind while creating a program or developing the marketing plan can allow program managers to engage with their stakeholders and adapt to their needs before they are even enrolled.

Determining program attributes. Pre-college program managers need to understand the attributes of their program and be able to explain them to both stakeholders and external parties. Rigorous and relevant course work is an important element of a pre-college program but the out-of-class time elements should not be discounted. These elements—such as social life on campus, extracurricular activities, student health and wellness—rely on a diverse and engaging student body to drive success. Once you have identified your program attributes, you can create a persona and identify target audiences.

Recruiting relationships. While marketing techniques such as search engine optimization (SEO) and organic content marketing can help fill a pre-college cohort, traditional partnerships can play an important role in creating a balanced cohort and help programs find students who can be successful in the program. Community based organizations (CBOs), traditional educational partners, and grant funded scholarship programs are all examples of potential partners. These partners can help identify students who would be a good fit for the program and/or may not have previously had the opportunity to attend. Creating opportunities to underserved student populations may also align with the goals of the undergraduate admissions office.

After each campus determines its own student composition, it can use partnerships to achieve their ideal student population. As with marketing, partnership management requires specialized skills. One useful tool when seeking partnerships is a simple checklist:

- Is there alignment around organizational values?
- Do both groups want similar outcomes for the student participants?

- Is there a similar definition of success and of how to measure that success?
- Have the two groups established clear roles and responsibilities?
- Do both organizations feel like it is a mutually beneficial relationship?

It can also be helpful to think of partnerships as a long-range investment that takes time and trust to nurture. One useful framework is Tuckman's (1965) Form, Storm, Norm, Conform process. It predicts that all partnerships—even those which meet the checklist above—will have a life cycle that includes the formation of the partnership, friction around shared decision making, and resetting of the partnership around new processes and improved performance. There are plenty of resources for those individuals interested in organizational psychology, but it is useful to point out two key takeaways that can be applied to both internal and external partnerships. The first is that it is normal to "storm" with a good partner. The second is that this cycle will continue while the partnership exists. In a long-term view of a partnership, both parties should measure success by their ability to spot the storm, fix it, and get back to a new level of performance.

Partnership with undergraduate admissions. Admissions offices often embrace innovation and new ideas. As universities grow their pre-college programs, the opportunity exists for pre-college program managers to create mutually beneficial relationships with admissions offices and leverage resources. Undergraduate admissions offices can benefit from traditional pre-recruitment tactics including admissions presentations and recruitment literature. Both admissions offices and pre-college programs can also benefit from the sharing of marketing resources including lists.

Ackerman and Schibrowksy (2007) first suggested applying the business concept of relationship marketing as a means of student retention. This concept can also be applied to work done through the collaboration between undergraduate admissions and pre-college programs. Ackerman and Schibrowsky (2007) pulled from the relationship marketing theory to conclude

> *"commitment serves as a measure of how important to both parties the relationship is and their mutual willingness to continue it. In terms of student relationship marketing, it is proposed that students who perceive a mutual and strong commitment between themselves and the college are more likely to remain enrolled and are more likely to recommend the school to friends"* (p. 320).

Instilling a commitment in students from their time as pre-college students can carry over to their undergraduate experience and even their involvement as alumni.

Conclusion
Overall, pre-college programs can offer numerous benefits to their host institutions and create a pipeline of engaged students from prospect to alumni. Pre-college program managers can advocate for programs by carefully understanding their institution's goals from various perspectives, most importantly from the viewpoint of key decision makers. The encouragement from these campus leaders will stimulate institutional support across campus, leading to increased program success rates and added value to the various on-campus units. Faculty and department involvement and a continued strategic partnership with the admissions office will also assist pre-college program managers in their role of keeping students in the pipeline. To summarize, pre-college

programs can offer a high value student an extended, immersive marketing experience, prepare them for the rigors of life at the university, and help the university learn more about a student over the course of the program.

About the Authors

Dr. Meghan Groome is the Director of the Pre-College Division at The School of the New York Times. Previously she was Senior Vice President for Education at the New York Academy of Sciences, where she oversaw a global portfolio of education programs including numerous National Science Foundation Grants.

Kacey McCaffrey is the Senior Program Manager of Student Life at The School of The New York Times and oversees policy development, risk management, and student life operations across The School's programs for pre-college students. She is also an active member of the national Pre-College Program Directors group.

REFERENCES

Ackerman, R., & Schibrowsky, J. (2007). A business marketing strategy applied to student retention: A higher education initiative. *Journal of College Student Retention, 9*(3), 307–336. doi:10.2190/CS.9.3.d

Belkin, D. (2019, Jan. 26). Colleges mine data on their applicants; to determine 'demonstrated interest,' some schools are tracking how quickly prospective students open email and whether they click links. *The Wall Street Journal.* Retrieved from https://www.wsj.com/articles/the-data-colleges-collect-on-applicants-11548507602

Hisanabe, Y. (2009, April). Persona marketing for Fujitsu Kids Site. *FUJITSU Scientific & Technical Journal, 45*(2), 210–218. Retrieved from http://www.fujitsu.com/global/documents/about/resources/publications/fstj/archives/vol45-2/paper07.pdf

International Town & Gown Association. (2019). Retrieved from https://www.itga.org/

Kinzie, J., & Kuh, G. (2004). Going deep: Learning from campuses that share responsibility for student success. *About Campus, 9*(5), 2–8. doi:10.1002/abc.105

Kramer, G. L. (2007). *Fostering student success in the campus community.* San Francisco, CA: Jossey-Bass.

Marcus, J. (2017, May 1). Under pressure to contain tuition, colleges scramble for other revenue. Retrieved from https://www.washingtonpost.com/news/grade-point/wp/2017/05/01/under-pressure-to-contain-tuition-colleges-scramble-for-other-revenue/

Nordvall, R. C., & Braxton, J. M. (1996). An alternative definition of quality of undergraduate college education: Toward usable knowledge for improvement. *The Journal of Higher Education, 67*(5), 483–497. doi:10.2307/2943865

Perna, M. C. (2005). The enrollment funnel. *Techniques: Connecting Education and Careers, 80*(8), 36–37. Retrieved from https://eric.ed.gov/?id=EJ720796

Thomasian, J. (2011, Dec.). *Building a science, technology, engineering, and math education agenda: An update of state actions.* Washington, DC: National Governors Association. Retrieved from https://files.eric.ed.gov/fulltext/ED532528.pdf

Tinto, V. (2006). Research and practice of student retention: What next? *Journal of College Student Retention: Research, Theory & Practice, 8*(1), 1–19. doi:10.2190/4YNU-4TMB-22DJ-AN4W

Tuckman, B. W (1965). Developmental sequence in small groups. *Psychological Bulletin, 63*(6), 384–399. doi:10.1037/h0022100

U.S. Department of Health and Human Services. (n.d.) *Personas.* Retrieved from https://www.usability.gov/how-to-and-tools/methods/personas.html

Chapter 8

Pre-College as Experiential Education and Immersive Learning

By Susie Sheldon Rush and William Alba, Ph.D.
Carnegie Mellon University

Pre-college programs challenge participants to develop as intellectual social beings through new experiences. Kolb's experiential learning model provides a framework for how this development occurs both in and out of the classroom, by informing how learners actively engage in, reflect upon, conceptualize, and resolve their experiences. In this chapter, we present examples and case studies to elucidate how experiential education and immersive experiences anchor pre-college transformational learning outcomes. We demonstrate how not only students but also staff, faculty, and families are involved in and benefit from the pre-college experience. Finally, we explore how to develop systems that build student resilience in order to transform potential failure into opportunities for success.

Theoretical Framework

The theory of experiential education provides a lens to understand pre-college learning. David Kolb's Experiential Learning Theory (ELT) describes a four-stage cycle in which learners engage through Concrete Experience, Reflective Observation, Abstract Conceptualization, and Active Experimentation. These four dimensions are coupled in diametrically opposed poles: the conceptual and the operational. In Kolb's theory, both the conceptual and operational must exist to develop a transformative learning experience. Because the four-stage process is cyclical, not linear, learners may enter at different stages and move among them. In addition, since learners come to the process with their own sets of previous experiences, they each have their own style of engaging with the four stages (Kolb, 1984).

Pre-college programs offer a special opportunity for students to develop along Kolb's four stages through immersion in the unique environment of higher education. Immersive experiences give individuals opportunities to engage in a hands-on learning process that allows for transformational outcomes: "All learning is experiential but some experiential contexts are more challenging and are richer in their potential to engage people in ways that change them" (Jackson, 2008, p. 5). For example, immersion in a language culture helps learning occur faster and more effectively: "[Experience-based learning] aids language learning by placing it in a context and culture" (Boud, 2008, p. 9).

Similarly, by living in a college setting, pre-college learners are immersed in the context and culture of higher education. This immersion focuses the majority of their attention on the lived educational experience and helps them to become independent self-advocates, understand college norms, gain confidence, develop life skills, and navigate life in college and beyond. As we will explore later in the chapter, crisis experiences, although difficult, can also provide an unconventional opportunity for transformational learning.

Carnegie Mellon University Pre-College Program
The Pre-College Program at Carnegie Mellon University in 2018 comprised eight academic programs: five within the College of Fine Arts (Architecture, Art, Design, Drama, Music),

one directed by the Entertainment Technology Center (National High School Game Academy), a new program focused on Artificial Intelligence, and a program that offered college courses from across the university (Advanced Placement Early Admission Program – APEA). That summer there were 538 students enrolled, including 498 living in campus housing, 90 of whom were international students. While each of these and other summer high-school programs at the university provides experiential learning opportunities, the focus in this chapter is on the APEA Program, which was the largest at 220 students, as well as on the student life experience. The intention of the Carnegie Mellon University Pre-College program is to give students a transformative experience so that they may grow and make informed decisions about their educational aspirations.

In the APEA Program, we expect pre-college students to self-advocate, make decisions, and problem-solve on their own. Because pre-college students are minors, we are especially mindful of cultivating a supportive environment. The APEA grade redaction policy is one example of how we create an environment that is simultaneously supportive, autonomous, and low-risk. Any APEA student who participates fully and meets the faculty member's standard for student engagement is permitted to redact that course and grade from their transcript. This allows students to fully engage with the course material and the holistic pre-college experience without the potential outcome of a low grade that could negatively impact their college admission. Academic advising, periodic check-ins, and connecting students to necessary resources are additional examples of crucial elements for developing a robust and supportive learning environment.

How pre-college provides "everyday" experiential education opportunities for:

Students

One of the most significant challenges that students and their families encounter in a pre-college program is adjusting from high-school to college norms, such as the significantly reduced level of parent access to the student's educational records, the higher expectation for students to be self-motivated and advocate for themselves, and the greater expectation of student independence. We are therefore intentional about helping students and their families understand and navigate an educational setting in which the responsibility of learning is centered on the student.

This student-centered development often begins before a student applies to the program, during the fall, winter, and spring when students and their families are learning about and considering various summer opportunities. When parents inquire about the APEA Program to help their children choose from a slate of approximately 40 college courses, the administrators ask to speak directly with the student instead. This reinforces the norm, for both students and families, that the student is in charge of their own learning. Based on Kolb's framework, this way of advising the students about course selection constitutes an opportunity for Reflective Observation: the student is reflecting on their past experiences and evaluating their own readiness to engage with the subject.

After students apply to the program and are admitted, they receive information in order to manage electronic student services, including their academic records; email accounts; course syllabuses, grades, and assignments; and other privileged information. Although we know that students sometimes share their usernames and passwords with their parents, this is solely at the discretion of the student. This is another example of how the customary high-school practice of sharing information with families does not match the practices that the student and family will shortly face when the student is enrolled in college. Viewed through the lens of Kolb's Experiential Learning Theory, the act of logging in and experiencing the enrollment process, either by themselves or with their parent(s)/guardian(s), maps to the Active Experimentation module. In this step, students and parents are beginning to be exposed to college norms and may start to realize that those norms are different from high school norms.

During opening weekend presentations and throughout the six-week program, the academic director, student affairs director, professors, and staff endeavor to manage the expectations of faculty-student and faculty-parent interactions, which are also different from patterns commonly found in high schools. The credit-bearing college courses are taught in ways that demand and foster a greater degree of independent learning. For example, students are often surprised to discover that college work provides more free time outside the classroom than high school, and then surprised again when they find that they must become more self-disciplined in using that time for their studies. They learn the value of office hours, the practice of identifying the areas of their own lack of knowledge, and the art of asking precise questions. For students who were the star pupils in their respective schools, they come to terms with the fact that they may need additional support in the college environment. They experiment with living college norms, including navigating where and how to ask for help. They may engage resources such as Academic

Development, Disability Resources, and Counseling and Psychological Services. Fortunately, resident advisors, who are current undergraduates at the university, can help students navigate the unfamiliar territory and serve as role models.

Families

Families are sometimes caught off-guard that professors do not reach out when their children are doing poorly, and to learn that they are legally obligated not to do so. This surprise occurs because, in most secondary schools, the educational record accrues to the parent/guardian. In contrast, this is not necessarily true for students who are enrolled in an institution of higher education. Contrary to the expectations of families, they are no longer equal partners in their child's educational enterprise. Instead, the ownership is centered on the child. This bewilderment can exist despite receiving information about FERPA (the Family Educational Rights and Privacy Act) in application materials, enrollment forms, and during opening weekend. The university's interpretation of FERPA coupled with the policy for the Protection of Minors can become complex. The experience of working through this delicate balance can inform both the student and family on college norms regarding FERPA. In addition, faculty and staff receive experience in communicating those norms.

Case Study 1:
Student Admission and Enrollment

One benefit of students participating in any Pre-College program around the country is the transition from high school norms to college norms. Through the admission and enrollment process, Pre-College programs can provide many experiential education opportunities for students and families to understand the expectations of self-advocacy and independence.

Simon is in his junior year of high school and has decided that he wants to attend a Pre-College program this summer. He expressed his interest to his parents and they thought it was a great idea. Simon's parents are very invested in his education, having served on numerous committees at his high school. They are quite ingrained in the high school's culture and have a great deal of experience advocating on behalf of students.

Naturally, when Simon expressed interest in attending a Pre-College program, his parents were enthusiastic to be involved in the process. Simon's parents sat down with him one fall evening in order to submit an application to the Pre-College program. The application asked for an email address and the parents entered their family email address so that they could also be informed as to the admission decision. This email address is managed by Simon's parents.

When the email arrived notifying Simon of his acceptance to the program, the whole family was thrilled. They began making their plans for Simon to attend the 6-week Pre-College program. As part of the enrollment process, Simon was asked to request the courses that he would like to take. The enrollment materials noted that some courses fill quickly and encouraged students to complete the course request as soon as possible.

Since the education process has always been a family affair in Simon's world, his parents had many questions about the content of what he would be learning, the pace of the courses, if he would be earning college credit, and more. Simon's parents decided to call the administrative offices to inquire about the courses, assignments, structure, and student life experience.

The program director was happy to speak with Simon's parents about general aspects of the program so that they felt confident and comfortable in sending Simon to the program. However, the director encouraged Simon to become part of the conversation. The director explained how their institution interprets the Federal Education Rights Privacy Act (FERPA) laws related to higher education in that the educational record belongs solely to the student when enrolled in this institution of higher education.

Furthermore, the director wanted to get Simon engaged in the conversation as a developmental opportunity for Simon to be in charge of his own educational path. Simon and his parents were beginning to learn the expectations and path toward development by participating in the Pre-College program.

At their family dinner that night, Simon and his parents discussed the need for Simon to communicate directly with the Pre-College program about his experience and educational path at the Pre-College program. They determined as a family that it would be best for Simon to consult with his parents, but be the one to communicate directly with the Pre-College program.

After the conversation with his parents, Simon retreated to his room in order to read through the Student Handbook that had been sent by the program and understand more about what his experience would be. Lying in bed that night, Simon imagined what it would be like to visit office hours, meet with his TAs, and explore the city with some future new friends that he would make in the program.

As a result, Simon began to develop his own independence, self-discovery, and self-advocacy. The next day, Simon changed his email address in his student record to his own personal email address instead of the family address so that he could receive communication directly and later loop in his parents as necessary or desired. Simon also wrote an email to the director in order to acquire his course schedule for the summer.

One point of emphasis is that we do not advocate for cutting the parents out of the process entirely. Instead, it is better to have the student take the lead on their own educational path. Communication with parents is critical in terms of general program information; however, helping Pre-College students to develop skills in their own right is equally important.

Through this commonplace experience, Simon and his family had an opportunity for experiential learning that enhanced Simon and his family's development. If we view this situation through the lens of Kolb's theory, we can match the Concrete Experience phase to Simon's parents taking the action of reaching out to the Pre-College program on Simon's behalf. The Reflective Observation phase relates to the conversation that Simon had with his parents at their family dinner. They were able to reflect on the reasons why it would be beneficial for Simon to become more involved in the process. Abstract Conceptualization happened when Simon was imagining what his experience would be like when he is taking the initiative, like meeting with TAs and exploring the city. Finally, the Active Experimentation phase is exemplified by Simon changing his email address in his student record and emailing the director to test out his newly acquired skills.

Case Study 2:
Resident Advisor Training

The role of Resident Advisor (RA) itself provides robust, experience-based learning opportunities for staff. Not only are the RAs supporting and supervising the pre-college students, but they are also engaging in an experiential learning opportunity of their own. Undergraduate CMU students apply to and are selected for this unique employment opportunity. This experience-based learning for the RAs can be exemplified by their training.

Prior to training, RAs are expected to review their job responsibilities thoroughly so that they can come to training week with an appropriate foundation. This is an example of Abstract Conceptualization in Kolb's model. Throughout the week of training, the RAs will have interactive sessions on topics such as mandated reporting, bystander intervention, conflict resolution, and operational aspects of their job. This also constitutes Abstract Conceptualization. RAs participate in small group debrief sessions in which they can reflect and ask questions about what they have learned that day, which maps to the Reflective Observation mode of Kolb's model. The final training session is a hands-on experience used by many Resident Assistant training programs called Behind Closed Doors. In this activity, Pre-College RAs role-play difficult situations and resolve them based on their training. This gives RAs opportunities to test their skills in a low-risk setting before the students arrive. After each role-play, the group reflects on the situation. This satisfies the Active Experimentation as well as Reflective Observation modes of Kolb's model. Lastly, as the early arrival students begin to arrive, the RAs are using the Concrete Experience mode of Kolb's model. RAs are encouraged to reflect often on their experience through weekly one-on-one and ad hoc meetings with their supervisor.

Depending on each individual RA's learning style, they may experience these opportunities differently. Typically, the RAs report that the Behind Closed Doors role-playing session brought their learning to life and they were able to put their learning into context. The immersive experience was able to give them the opportunity to contextualize and practice their new skills. Image 1 gives a visual representation that connects the RA staff training to their experiential education process.

Image 1.
Pre-College RA Staff Training Experiential Education Process.

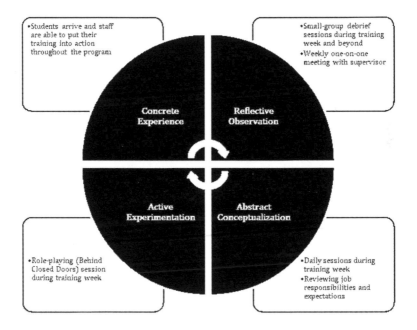

•Students arrive and staff are able to put their training into action throughout the program

•Small-group debrief sessions during training week and beyond
•Weekly one-on-one meeting with supervisor

Concrete Experience

Reflective Observation

Active Experimentation

Abstract Conceptualization

•Role-playing (Behind Closed Doors) session during training week

•Daily sessions during training week
•Reviewing job responsibilities and expectations

Students, families, faculty, and staff are all involved in the experiential education process. In Image 2, we categorize some experiences that can lead to experiential education. Of course, all programs are different and may provide different experiences for learners. The blank boxes in the table illustrate the opportunity to create more circumstances for experiential learning.

Image 2.
Pre-College Sample Experiences --> Experiential Education.

	Students	Families	Faculty	Residential Staff
Before Program	• Advising for course selection • Review enrollment materials	• Communication with families to explain college norms including FERPA		• Training • Presence of pre-college student alums who seek RA experience
Opening	• Presentation of rules and regulations • Move-in • Finding classrooms prior to the first day of class	• Expectation to stay connected, but allow students to explore and test on their own	• Understand differences in pre-college learning (pace, physiological differences, differences from home environment • Recognize differences in motivation and preparation of pre-college students and undergraduates	• Leadership experience - leading large group events and activities during orientation, supervising and advising floor community
During Program	• Utilizing and navigating resources • Crisis (failing exams, academic integrity violations, behavioral violations)	• During day-to-day interactions understanding how FERPA may apply	• Providing college academic norms for pre-college students	• Advising pre-college students on college norms • Receive performance evaluations • Reflect on how to leverage RA experience for future employment
After Program	• Receive grades • Grade redaction		• Recommendation letters for some students	

While students, families, faculty, and staff are all involved in the process, the center of the learning is on the student. It is important that the focus of the experiences and outcomes are based on the best interest of the student, with the families, faculty, and staff taking on a support role. This is particularly relevant in crisis situations.

Pre-College Crisis Situations as Experiential Education Opportunities

Experiential learning in pre-college summer programs can occur not only in the normal course of events; sometimes the most transformative learning opportunities arise when students are in crisis. Despite active engagement and risk management, crisis situations will inevitably occur. During a crisis situation, the primary objective is student support and safety. However, these situations can also be excellent experiential learning opportunities. In fact, the very act of supporting students can lead to learning.

These crisis circumstances heighten the stakes as well as awareness of *Experiencing, Reflecting, Conceptualizing, and Testing* for everyone involved with the student's education: faculty, staff, families, and of course the student. When a student is in crisis, such that their safety or enrollment in the program is in serious question, all hands are on deck. The most important aspect of these situations is that the pre-college staff and faculty handle the situation with dignity, respect, integrity, and focus the outcomes on student growth. We will now explore a hypothetical student crisis situation in which a pre-college student is found to be guilty of an academic integrity violation.

Case Study 3:
Academic Integrity Crisis

When Margaret enrolled in the APEA Pre-College Program at Carnegie Mellon, she had no intention of committing an academic integrity violation. However, she was unaccustomed to the demanding and fast-paced work in her two pre-college credit-bearing courses and found herself struggling. Margaret wanted it to seem as though she was able to keep pace, so she did not ask for help when she started falling behind with her coursework.

Margaret called Andrew, her friend from home who had attended the CMU Pre-College program the prior year. Margaret knew that Andrew had excelled in the same Math class with the same professor, Dr. Morrison. Andrew agreed to help Margaret try to understand the material. As the week progressed, Margaret had a problem set due on Friday but she still was not able to fully grasp the material. Margaret asked Andrew to write the proof for her. Margaret thought that although she might fail an exam, she would still have As on the homework. At best, Margaret thought she could earn a C in the class. Andrew agreed to help, against his better judgement. Margaret submitted the proofs that Andrew wrote for her the following day as her own work.

Dr. Morrison received a tip from another student that Margaret had a friend who was writing some proofs on her assignment. After further research into Margaret and Andrew's answers, the professor confirmed that Margaret's proof was almost identical to Andrew's from the previous year.

Margaret initially claimed they were her own work, denying that she had violated course and university academic

_____

policies. She then recanted and reported that a friend had helped her.

The administrators involved agreed that the extent of Margaret and Andrew's unauthorized assistance and cheating were more-than-sufficient grounds for Margaret to fail the course and subsequently be expelled from the program. In addition, there could be consequences to Andrew's role in the violation. The administrators realized that this was a perfect opportunity to create space and awareness for Margaret to have a meaningful transformation through the experiential education process. The administrators developed a sanction plan wherein if Margaret remained enrolled, she would be required to complete all of the remaining assignments, exams, and projects, but would nevertheless fail the course based on the academic integrity violation. The only other outcome would be for Margaret to be expelled from the program.

The act and recognition of the academic integrity violation maps to the Concrete Experience mode of Kolb's theory. Subsequently, Margaret has the opportunity for Reflective Observation, through conversation with the APEA Director and the Counseling Center in the following days. The Abstract Conceptualization phase happens through conversations with the administrators about discussing this circumstance with her family, what the implications are, and how that will affect her moving forward. The Active Experimentation happens as she continues to work through the class, and how to properly seek the help she needs in order to understand the course material.

Ultimately, Margaret remained enrolled in the program, failed the course, and had some very difficult conversations with her family, the APEA Director, Andrew, and Dr. Morrison.

The plan to keep Margaret enrolled coupled with the developmental conversations were key factors in providing the environment and context for experiential learning.

At the end of the summer, Margaret expressed gratitude for being afforded the opportunity to develop as a person during the summer program. While this was not an ideal outcome for Margaret nor the instructor, this situation provided an opportunity for the cycle of experiential learning.

Conclusion
Pre-college programs enable students to experience college before they complete high school. This immersive experience allows students, families, staff, and faculty to engage in many experiential learning opportunities through their engagement with the program.

The pre-college immersive experience both cultivates and demands that students and families adapt from high school norms to college norms. The cultural, social, and legal aspects of these college norms shift the center of responsibility of education on the student, rather than on their families. Pre-college programs help students to adapt to college norms so that they become more self-aware and become stronger self-advocates, including along the stages illustrated by the Kolb Experiential Learning Theory (ELT) of Concrete Experience, Reflective Observation, Abstract Conceptualization, and Active Experimentation.

This chapter presented three case studies, leaning upon the Kolb model to contextualize how pre-college experiences and environments foster adaptation to college norms. We described how this important adjustment occurs not only for students and families, but also for staff and faculty working within a pre-college program. In our first case study, we focused on how admission, advising, and course enrollment processes help students and families acclimate to college. The next case study attended to how the Kolb model maps onto the training of resident advisor staff members in pre-college programs. Our final case study reflected on how students, faculty, administrators, and staff can help a student in the crisis situation of an academic integrity violation.

Pre-college administrators are well-positioned to construct and support educational structures and processes for students, in order to foster experiences that lead to positive developmental outcomes. Analyzing your own program through the perspective of experiential education can help to identify opportunities to enhance learning. We encourage our colleagues in this field to reflect upon their own experiences in pre-college education, conceptualize what they have accomplished, and continue to experiment with ways to improve their respective programs. While we have tabulated some ways that work in our own pre-college community, there inevitably remain gaps in our practice and the circumstances in our institution will vary from your own. We look forward to continuing this conversation, to learn of other ways to enhance pre-college through the lenses of experiential education and immersive learning.

About the Authors

Susie Sheldon Rush is the Director of Pre-College Programs at Carnegie Mellon University. She has worked in non-profit organizations and youth programs for 17 years, focusing on enhancing organizational structure and efficiency, as well as student/staff development and success. Susie currently serves on the Advisory Board for the national Pre-College Program Directors organization.

William Alba, Ph.D., is Director of the Advanced Placement Early Admission Program, the largest pre-college program at Carnegie Mellon University, where he also serves as Associate Dean for Diversity in the Mellon College of Science, Director of the Science and Humanities Scholars Program, and Associate Teaching Professor of Chemistry. He has founded and directed programs at the intersection between secondary school and higher education for more than a quarter century.

REFERENCES

Boud, D. (2008). Locating immersive experience in experiential learning. In *Appreciating the Power of Immersive Experience* (pp. 9–19). University of Surrey, Guildford: Surrey Centre for Excellence in Professional Training and Education. http://complexworld.pbworks.com/f/CONFERENCE%20PROGRAMME.pdf

Jackson, N. (2008). The Power of Immersive Experience. In *Appreciating the Power of Immersive Experience* (pp. 5–8). University of Surrey, Guildford: Surrey Centre for Excellence in Professional Training and Education. http://complexworld.pbworks.com/f/CONFERENCE%20PROGRAMME.pdf

Kolb, A. Y., & Kolb, D. A. (2017). *The experiential educator: Principles and practices of experiential learning.* Kaunakakai, HI: EBLS Press.

Kolb, D. A. (1984). *Experiential learning: Experience as the source of learning and development.* Englewood Cliffs, NJ: Prentice-Hall.

Chapter 9

Risk Management, Compliance, and Other Considerations

By Lindsay Meyer Bond,
The Ohio State University

Many recent and horrific situations in higher education involving the maltreatment of minors have not only put minors at risk, but have also paralyzed institutions. Jerry Sandusky and Larry Nassar are two of the most prominent names known, but there are countless other perpetrators as well. A 2014 compilation of selected claims of child abuse, child neglect, and child pornography involving individuals associated with American college and universities (Franke, 2014) is 21 pages long, goes back only a few years, and does not even include all known situations. To say that this can happen anywhere at any time is an understatement. This compilation also only includes abuse, but there are countless other risks associated with working with youth, including medical management, authorized pick-ups, false allegations, and everything in between. But the pre-college programs in our universities are doing wonderful outreach and providing valuable services, so how do we protect those vulnerable students coming to us, as well as ourselves?

Applicable Laws and Other Regulations

The first place to start in managing risk and ensuring compliance is cataloging local, state, and national laws and regulations. Does the college or university have a protection of minors policy? Many institutions do now, and components of these policies and programs are addressed later in this chapter. But make this area the starting place, as these policies will already have state and federal laws taken into consideration.

Many states have laws related to working with youth, whether it be childcare centers, camps, or a multitude of activities. For instance, in Pennsylvania, there are countless laws related to the protection of youth, including HB 1276 (Act 15 of 2015), which requires that all adult volunteers and employees who work with children must obtain a criminal background check and child abuse clearance (Pennsylvania Department of Human Services, n.d.). But next door in Ohio, very few people working with children are required by law to obtain a criminal background check. In Texas, youth programs on campus are actually defined and all individuals working in programs on campuses of higher education are required to be trained on how to recognize signs of sexual abuse and molestation (2 Tex. Education Code, Ch. 22, 2007; 2 Tex. Education Code, Ch. 38, 2017; 3 Tex. Education Code, Ch. 51, 2011). Childwelfare.gov has a helpful breakdown by state on laws pertaining to reporting and responding to child abuse and neglect, maintaining child abuse and neglect records, protecting children from domestic violence, and related issues (Child Welfare Information Gateway, 2018).

There are also national laws that program directors may need to be familiar with, such as the Family Educational Rights and Privacy Act (FERPA), Child Online Privacy Protection Act (COPPA), Child Protection Improvements Act (CPIA), Americans with Disabilities Act (ADA), and the Protecting Young Victims from Sexual Abuse and Safe Sport Authorization Act of 2017.

While most individuals in higher education are at least aware of FERPA, there can be a grey area when it comes to pre-college programming. In general, FERPA protects the privacy of student education records. But does it apply to non-matriculated minors involved in youth programs? Leading experts within the American Association of Collegiate Registrars and Admissions Officers (AACRAO) and the National Association of College and University Attorneys (NACUA) have interpreted that FERPA applies to participants in non-credit programs, while some universities have considered these programs to be out of scope. There is not a clear national consensus yet, so a conversation with each institution's general counsel would be advised.

The Child Online Privacy Protection Act (COPPA) aims to protect children's safety and privacy on the internet by imposing regulations when it comes to collecting information of children under 13 years of age (Federal Trade Commission, 1998). The goal is to limit the collection of personally identifiable information from children under the age of 13 without their parents' consent.

The Child Protection Improvements Act (CPIA) is a bipartisan-backed law that provides youth-serving organizations interacting with children and other vulnerable populations — such as the elderly and individuals with disabilities—with access to Federal Bureau of Investigation (FBI) fingerprint background checks to screen prospective employees and volunteers. It is supposed to expedite the amount of time in which results are obtained, lower costs, and increase accuracy (American Camp Association, 2018). Details of implementation are still being worked out, but this is one to keep on the radar to determine what implications may be.

If a program is open to the general public and a minor with a disability wants to participate, the Americans with Disabilities Act (ADA) will be applicable. This Act is a civil rights law that prohibits discrimination against individuals with disabilities (United States Department of Justice Civil Rights Division, n.d.). See the campus ADA/Section 504 coordinator for more education if needed.

The Safe Sport Act aims to prevent the sexual abuse of minors, including amateur athletes, by requiring abuse reporting (Protecting Young Victims from Sexual Abuse and Safe Sport Authorization Act of 2017). This is a fairly new law, with a lot of inconsistent interpretation. This is another one that is worth a legal consult.

These laws are not the only regulations when it comes to working with minors. Due diligence in seeking out laws and regulations is a key first step in protecting minors and those interacting with them.

Identifying Areas of Potential Risk

While knowledge of laws and regulations is vital to managing risk and ensuring compliance, it is also imperative to identify where potential risk lives, and who is responsible for mitigating it. Sexual predators need privacy, access, and control in order to groom and molest a victim. Situations where this trifecta can be established are very risky and should be avoided. The Gallagher report (Arthur J. Gallagher & Co., 2012) further outlines an analysis of risk in what to "worry about most," as well as a loss control measures scoring sheet. From the obvious risks of alcohol and drugs to inadequate forms (including waivers, emergency contact information, medical authorization forms) being collected, there are many risks in working with minors. While not all may result in abuse, it is still important to consider the following factors when interacting with minors:

Responsibility
- o The first question to ask is who is responsible for the program, activity, and/or event? This might seem like an obvious question, but is it always simple? What about when the minors are visiting other areas of campus, going on field trips, visiting a lab, etc.? It should be clear who is responsible for the minors and when, so that risk can be managed properly. Additionally, if something happens, it is helpful to have this determined in advance.

Supervision
- o A big area of potential risk is inadequate supervision, and is the most common lawsuit in recreational programming (Cotten & Wolohan, 2017). This is especially challenging in pre-college programming because not many 15-, 16-, and 17-year-olds want to be actively supervised. It can be difficult to find a balance between knowing where minors are at all times and providing them with a "real" college experience, which includes freedom. However, the bottom line is that a minor is a minor by law, and they are entrusted to the university's care. Colleges and universities are so different from participants' high schools in that colleges and universities are open environments, whereas high schools are not. Take this situation as an example: An individual described as a "serial groper" was accessing property of a university and groping unassuming females across campus. He would be arrested, go to jail, and come right back (as well as to other venues). If the engineering camper is not supervised at all

times so that she can go study on her own like college students do, and the "serial groper" shows up, who is protecting this child? If a child is properly supervised at all times, there is no access to that child even if a bad apple does show up. Appropriate supervision is often obtained by proper training of staff and appropriate ratios of staff to children. American Camp Association guidelines (American Camp Association, 2018) are most recognized and recommended.

Unplanned time

- o Unplanned time is another area that is particularly challenging for pre-college programming and older youth. Most programmers want to allow program participants the dignity of attending to their own life and schedule, but again, they are legally entrusted to the care of the university. Planning the program properly, including limiting downtime, is an easy way to manage risk by eliminating the opportunity for alternatives that are less desirable.

Mixed age groups

- o Mixed age groups is a risk when the activity level or space is not appropriate for multiple ages, as well as the potential for peer-on-peer abuse. Peer-on-peer abuse is any abuse that occurs in which both the perpetrator and victim are minors. Oftentimes one perceives child abuse as a situation where an adult is mistreating a child, but the perpetrator can be a child as well. These situations can be tricky because the perpetrator may also be a victim of abuse. Bullying can fit within this category, along with exploitation; physical, sexual and emotional abuse; and even neglect. Those working in youth programming in the United States are seeing the increase in peer-on-peer abuse first-hand (Praesidium, 2019). The age gap in pre-college programming is not normally vast, but with the increase in reported peer-on-peer abuse coupled with this not being at the forefront of many minds, additional focus on the need for proper supervision and planned time is important.

Medical management

o   Medical management is more than how to care for a sick child, but encompasses knowing how (and when) to communicate regarding communicable diseases, dispensing medication (over the counter and prescription), addressing and perhaps accommodating mental health issues, handling medical emergencies, and much more. This is often not something that can be handled effectively "on the spot" and must be planned and communicated in advance.

Emergency management

o   Most colleges and universities are well-versed in emergency management as it relates to matriculated college students. How do these plans change when it involves youth, from the actual execution of securing a space to communication to parents?

Transportation, drop-off, pick-up procedures

o   All transportation procedures pose challenges and are often an after-thought to program planning. If staff or volunteers are transporting, are they covered under university insurance, trained, avoiding one-on-one interactions (including the first child picked up and last dropped off), and is vehicle maintenance appropriately handled? Are personnel responsible for the minors when they arrive on campus or when they enter the building? A lawsuit may argue that the responsibility begins when the parent drops them off, but if there are no drop-off and pick-up procedures, this results in a major risk gap. There are custody battles and authorized pick-ups to consider, as well as a lack of supervision from drop-off to program location. Knowing that a predator needs privacy, access, and control, the situation would be ripe for misconduct during these times. What if children drive themselves or ride-share to or from the activity or program, and it is not known who is expected to pick up the minor?

Physical space
- o Is the program in a space that is appropriate and safe for the age groups being served? Is it public or private? Are there opportunities for a predator to take a child or for youth to sneak off on their own or together? Are they allowed to go to the rest-room alone, and if so, how far away is it, who else could be in the building, and is it known when they get back?

Social media
- o This is a ripe area in which to consult with experts at each particular university. Think about if phones will be allowed, how staff and volunteers can or can-not contact program participants, how to respond to negative postings, snaps, and tweets, and all other social media challenges.

Abuse and neglect
- o The risk of a child being abused or neglected while entrusted to an individual's care is real, as is the ability to be a voice for a child who does not otherwise have one when abuse is occurring outside the program. It is important to recognize signs of physical, sexual, and emotional abuse and neglect, as well as how to report suspected abuse. If the institution does not have a reporting policy, the program should. Local police and child protection services should be alerted, and oftentimes campus police want to be in-the-know as well. Once a reporting process is established, it is imperative to train staff on the types of abuse, signs, and how to report suspected concerns. More information on this can be found in the resources at the end of the chapter.

Risk Treatment

Once risks are identified, the next step is to treat them. The goal of risk management is not to eliminate all of the risks, but rather to minimize risks without fundamentally altering the activity or program. When it comes to risk management, one often starts with the DIM process: develop, implement, and manage (Cotten & Wolohan, 2017). The first step is to develop a risk management plan, and there are likely experts on campus to help with this. Developing the plan consists of identifying the risks as outlined in the previous section, classifying the risk (as outlined in the Gallagher report), and selecting a method of treatment for each.

Risks can be treated by avoidance, transferring, accepting, and reducing. Avoidance is typically not the preferred method, but may need to be used for extremely dangerous risks or those that can be easily managed differently (i.e., can a lab with open doors be used when others are around instead of the one in the basement after hours? Does transportation HAVE to be part of the program, or can parents and guardians be provided with clear directions and parking, or information to public transportation, etc.)? Transferring can be done through insurance, third parties, and contracts. Insurance can help protect against some losses and may be appropriate in many cases. Contractual relationships, including with third parties, transfer relatable risks to that entity. Accepting a risk is appropriate when the risk is small and when physical and financial burden would not be extraordinary, such as the risk of a sprained ankle. Lastly, reduction of a risk can be accomplished through waivers and other forms. Consult with general counsel for the most appropriate forms.

When implementing a risk management plan, include all personnel who are involved with it to make them aware of the policies and procedures, put the treatment decisions into print, and train individuals on the entire plan and treatment. Designate an individual to manage and be responsible for the plan, and provide them with the authority to lead and execute, all while continually soliciting feedback and making tweaks. Cotten and Wolohan (2017) cover managing risk more extensively.

Components of a Youth Protection Program

As previously mentioned, many colleges and universities have policies and programs related to the protection of minors while entrusted to the institution's care. These policies can be brief, especially when state laws are strong or extensive. If the program is not in scope of a wider policy, consideration should be given to have one at the program level. Youth protection programs typically include the following components:

- Central repository of what is happening and where
  - Know where youth are and when, for reasons outlined in the identifying areas of risk section. It is difficult for a single person to compile this information, and it can be helpful to leverage partnerships across campus to identify where minors are in higher ed. Chupak, Weaver, and Bond (2019) outline a comprehensive table of all potential university partners that can assist in this endeavor.

- Reporting requirements (as discussed in identifying areas of risk section)

- Training of child abuse and neglect, risk management policies and other pertinent information (as discussed in identifying areas of risk and risk treatment sections)

- Background checks
  - Know state regulations, as the type of background checks differ greatly.

- Supervisory ratios (as discussed in identifying areas of risk section)

- Behavioral expectations, including a prohibition of one-on-one interactions
  - List what types of behaviors are expected from those working with youth, and consequences of violation so that expectations are very clear. Most institutions prohibit one-on-one interactions not only for the protection of the minor (think Jerry Sandusky and Larry Nassar), but for those working with the minors

as well. If a staff member is one-on-one with a minor and a false allegation is made against that individual, there is no alibi.

- Accountability
  - o Enforce expectations and see what is actually happening by being at the program as much as possible.

More information on youth protection policies can be found at Higher Education Protection Network (2019) and more details on building a youth protection program can be found in the referenced Chupak et al. (2019) article.

CHECKLIST
Components of a Youth Protection Program

☑	Component
	Central repository of what is happening and where
	Reporting requirements
	Training regarding child abuse and neglect
	Background checks
	Supervisory ratios
	Behavioral expectations, including a prohibition of one-on-one interactions
	Accountability

Establish and Maintain a Culture of Vigilance

Now that the parameters for managing the risks of working with youth are established, promoting compliance of policies and expectations is imperative. Individuals have been working with minors in higher education without any guidelines for a long time, so a change in culture is likely needed in order to establish buy-in, promote compliance, and identify this movement as a priority (Chupak et al., 2019). This can be done through management by walking around, in which staff and volunteers are managed by supervisors simply walking around, seeing what is going on, and when it is part of the culture to have ongoing monitoring, this can decrease the likelihood of misconduct. Engaging with individuals actually interacting with the youth is also imperative. Is the one-on-one prohibition even feasible? How is constant supervision actually occurring? How can barriers be removed? It is also important to remain in-the-know of current trends and incidents. Each incident should result in an internal review of policies and practices, which should be tweaked where needed. There are great resources listed in the next section.

Site visits are also important. While walking around, have a checklist and see if expectations are being met—from background checks to supervised transition times, and everything in between. Continual evaluation is critical, especially after an incident, no matter how strong the program is. When it comes to protecting youth, it is worth the time to look within to see how personnel can do better.

Buy-in for the protection of minors in pre-college programming is likely to fade over time if it is approached as a one-time checking of a box, but engaging with those interacting with the minors, raising awareness of current trends and incidents, and building and maintaining relationships with institutional partners are all successful methods in trying to prevent risk creep and incorporating this into an institution's culture (Chupak et al., 2019).

Summary

Whether the goal of a pre-college program is to recruit future students, to give back to the community, or simply to generate revenue in the summer, the responsibility of those caring for the youth does not change. The fact that a participant may be seventeen and coming to the institution as a full-time student in the fall does not change the level of responsibility required. It is a very fine line to balance in giving these students the college experience, which usually entails great amounts of freedom, while fulfilling legal or mandated responsibilities.

Individuals should first know their responsibilities under local, state, and national laws and regulations, specifically the Family Educational Rights and Privacy Act (FERPA), Child Online Privacy Protection Act (COPPA), Child Protection Improvements Act (CPIA), Americans with Disabilities Act (ADA), and Protecting Young Victims from Sexual Abuse and Safe Sport Authorization Act of 2017.

Risks in working with youth are everywhere. Who is responsible, and when, must be clear, and programs must adequately plan for and execute proper supervision, unplanned time, mixed age groups, medical and emergency management, transportation, pick-up and drop-off procedures, appropriate use of physical space, management of social media, and how to recognize signs of and report suspected or known abuse or neglect.

The before-mentioned risks should be enveloped in a risk management plan, with a treatment selected for each. This risk management plan could feasibly result in the creation of a youth protection program, whether at the institution level or program level. Youth protection programs usually involve a central repository of all youth activities, programs, and services, reporting requirements, training expectations, background check clearance, supervisory ratios, behavioral expectations and standards, and accountability measures.

Youth protection is a cultural movement, not a blip on the radar of reform in higher education. Those of us in higher education should continue to provide outstanding opportunities to the youth that are seeking them, as they are our future and we have much to teach them. However, outside of all the laws and policies outlined, we have a basic moral and ethical responsibility to help to ensure the safety and well-being of these individuals while entrusted to our care. We also have a profound opportunity to be a voice for a child who may not otherwise have one, and to be an advocate for them on all levels.

Resources

To make informed decisions and receive support from subject matter experts, youth programmers can turn to peer groups and organizations dedicated to the protection of minors on campus:

The Higher Education Protection Network (HEPNet) is a national association established in 2017 that seeks to promote positive interactions of higher education institutions with children and youth. Members serve as a coordinated voice promoting good practices for protecting vulnerable populations and providing programming and resources appropriate to their needs. More information can be found at higheredprotection.org.

The American Camp Association (ACA) is a national association that provides resources and development opportunities for youth protection specialists, administrators, program coordinators, and camp directors. A network within ACA known as "Camps on Campus" provides specialized content and resources for organizations and professionals who operate youth programs on college and university campuses. For more information, visit acacamps.org.

Regional and conference-based networks provide opportunities for programmers to benchmark with peer institutions.

About the Author

Lindsay Meyer Bond is the Youth Protection Program Consultant at The Ohio State University. Since 2014, Lindsay has directed and expanded Ohio State's Protection of Minors Policy to include over 40,000 individuals interacting with over 700,000 minors annually. Lindsay also serves as the Higher Education Protection Network's executive director and is an adjunct faculty member at Ohio State. Lindsay earned her B.A., M.Ed., and M.A. degrees from The Ohio State University.

REFERENCES

American Camp Association. (2018, March 26). *Child Protection Improvements Act becomes law*. Retrieved February 6, 2019, from https://www.acacamps.org/news-publications/hot-topic/child-protection-improvements-act-becomes-law

American Camp Association. (2018, December 10). *How to choose a camp: Safety tips*. Retrieved May 13, 2019, from https://www.acacamps.org/campers-families/planning-camp/preparing-camp/how-choose-camp-safety-tips

American Camp Association. (2019). Retrieved February 6, 2019, from https://www.acacamps.org/

Campus programs for minors. (2012, July 22). Retrieved February 11, 2019, from https://www.dshs.texas.gov/cpm/

Child Welfare Information Gateway. (2018). *Links to state and tribal child welfare law and policy*. Washington, DC: U.S. Department of Health and

---

Human Services, Children's Bureau. Retrieved February 6, 2019, from https://www.childwelfare.gov/topics/systemwide/laws-policies/can/

Chupak, D., Weaver, S., & Bond, L. M. (2019). Protection of minors in higher education programs: Emerging programs, policies, and practices. *Change: The Magazine of Higher Learning, 51* (2), 34–42. doi:10.1080/00091383.2019.1569971

Cotten, D. J., & Wolohan, J. T. (2017). *Law for recreation and sport managers* (7th ed.). Dubuque, IA: Kendall Hunt.

Family Educational Rights and Privacy Act, 20 U.S.C. § 1232g (1974).

Federal Trade Commission. (1998). Children's Online Privacy Protection Rule ("COPPA"). Retrieved February 6, 2019, from https://www.ftc.gov/enforcement/rules/rulemaking-regulatory-reform-proceedings/childrens-online-privacy-protection-rule

Franke, A. (2014, September 29). *Child abuse, child neglect, and child pornography situations involving higher education.* Retrieved February 6, 2019, from https://www.higheredprotection.org/s/Copy-of-20140929-Abuser-Molester-Chart-3grd.pdf

Arthur J. Gallagher & Co. (2012). Managing the risk of minors on campus. Retrieved from https://www.nccpsafety.org/assets/files/library/Managing_Risk_of_Minors_on_Campus.pdf

Higher Education Protection Network. (2019). Retrieved February 6, 2019, from https://www.higheredprotection.org/

Pennsylvania Department of Human Services. (n.d.) *Child Protective Services Laws.* Retrieved February 6, 2019, from http://keepkidssafe.pa.gov/about/cpsl/index.htm

Praesidium. (2019, May). *2019 Praesidium Report.* Retrieved May 20, 2019, from https://praesidium.lpages.co/praesidium-report-2019/

Protecting Young Victims from Sexual Abuse and Safe Sport Authorization Act of 2017, Pub. L. 115-126, § 534, Stat. 318. Retrieved February 6, 2019, from https://www.congress.gov/bill/115th-congress/senate-bill/534/text

2 Tex. Education Code Ch. 22. (2007, June 15). School district employees and volunteers. Retrieved February 11, 2019, from https://statutes. capitol.texas.gov/Docs/ED/htm/ED.22.htm

2 Tex. Education Code Ch. 38. (2017, June 12). Health and safety. Retrieved February 11, 2019, from https://statutes.capitol.texas.gov/ SOTWDocs/ED/htm/ED.38.htm

3 Tex. Education Code Ch. 51. (2011, September 1). Provisions generally applicable to higher education. Retrieved February 11, 2019, from https://statutes.capitol.texas.gov/Docs/ED/htm/ED.51.htm

United States Department of Justice Civil Rights Division. (n.d.). ADA.gov homepage. Retrieved February 6, 2019, from https://www.ada.gov/

Chapter 10

Pre-College as Outreach
Leveraging multi-unit support for effective, mission-based outreach with pre-college audiences

By Kari Storm, Bowling Green State University

Introduction

Pre-college outreach programs for youth are not often considered to be major focal points within institutions of higher education. Colleges and universities commonly align their strategic goals around the mission and needs of the institution. While not always absent from a university's mission, pre-college initiatives are seldom seen as an institutional priority. Therefore, encouraging buy-in from leaders and administrators within a university about the significance of pre-college work is usually met with a considerable amount of uncomfortable dissonance. Nathan Grawe, author of *Demographics and the Demand for Higher Education*, developed the HEDI, or the Higher Education Demand Index, which projects a 5% decrease of college age students by 2026 (Grawe, 2018). Grawe states:

> *"Demographic change is reshaping the population of the United States in ways that raise challenges for higher education. Through immigration, interstate migration, and fertility differences across demographic groups, the country's population is tilting toward the Southwest*

*in general and the Hispanic Southwest in particular.
From the perspective of the higher education sector,
these changes adversely shift the population away
from traditionally strong markets."* (Grawe, 2018, p. 6)

As tuition and education costs continue to rise, combined
with a changing college student demographic, it would be
remiss for universities to overlook the effects pre-college
programs as outreach have on students' post-enrollment
success in higher education. Through multi-unit collaborations and an intentional focus on linking youth programs
with faculty research and broader impacts, universities may
start to capitalize on—as well as reinforce—current student
competencies through involvement with the pre-college
programs. Universities have a dynamic opportunity when it
comes to engaging in outreach programs with pre-college
students, one that has the potential to serve all parties—
faculty, undergraduates, and pre-college affiliates.

Mission of Outreach

"Life's most persistent and urgent question is,
What are you doing for others?"
Martin Luther King, Jr. (Desiato, 2014)

Engaged pre-college outreach offers ample opportunities
for an institution to link both enrolled university students
alongside future students in altruistic efforts that help
strengthen and develop lifelong skills for both sides. One
area of such programming can be connected to offices of
service learning within institutions where undergraduate
students can volunteer with pre-college programs that offer
tutoring and mentoring opportunities. When universities
link service learning and volunteerism with pre-college
programs, a natural pathway develops between the two

entities. This engagement provides a direct pathway for pre-college students to see themselves as the college student volunteer who is working with them. The reward for volunteering and service learning has shown to have long-term effects on the undergraduate student as well. A study by Astin, Sax, and Avalos found that service learning participation encourages socialization across racial lines and increases commitment to promoting racial understanding in the years after college (Astin, Sax, & Avalos, 1999). One promising by-product university stakeholders can hope for, is that the study suggests there may be considerable institutional self-interest in encouraging students to participate in service work, as students who have experienced volunteering present a likelihood to return a monetary investment to their alma mater (Astin et al., 1999). A final area of impact that is often overlooked with pre-college programs is the program experience for the host (undergraduate student and faculty). In most university outreach programming models, undergraduate students and faculty serve as mentors while a department or college within the university serves as the host. Rebecca Blonshine examines in detail the effect of pre-college work on undergraduates; in her work, "Impact of Mentoring on Former Pre-College Program Participants: Gaining While Giving Back." She highlights that the undergraduate students felt purpose and value from sharing their experiences with and mentoring the high school students (Blonshine, 2014, p. 74).

Blonshine also states that:

"Participants (undergraduate students) expressed gaining several skills and knowledge from their work experience that assisted in their academic success at the university. The majority of the participants revealed that the communication and leadership skills they gained

from working for their pre-college program made them more confident to talk to their professors and ask for help when they needed tutoring services." (Blonshine, 2014, p. 76)

These secondary benefits observed within faculty and students who work with pre-college programs can be defined as the intended by-products of successful outreach programs. Such by-products can be measured in student retention, publications, and public awareness about the work of the faculty and university.

Types of Pre-College Outreach
For the purpose of understanding outreach as it pertains to pre-college students, there are three main categories into which programming can often be categorized. They include: 1) need-based, 2) awareness-based, and 3) information-based outreach programs.

 Need-based programs.
Need-based programs often develop as a way of answering a current problem facing a community or society in general. These programs focus on direct goals or outcomes that can be measured through programmatic assessments and evaluations that concentrate efforts on addressing or over-coming specific needs. Need-based programs can be connected to federal or state level grant funding with specific benchmarks in place in one or more areas, such as increasing student access to college, raising enrollment for under-rep-resented populations, or striving to increase diversity. A second aspect of need-based programming can be observed in communities where a direct need is not being met—such as access to mental health resources, clean water, or support centers for children/youth affected by the national opioid epidemic—and therefore elicits the attention of a

college or university to become involved with the community to address such deficiencies.

② *Awareness-based programs.*
Awareness-based programming can loosely be connected to need-based programs. With awareness-based outreach programs, institutions seek to raise awareness or promote services that are available for pre-college students to access. For instance, universities may develop partnerships with local school districts to build after-school tutoring programs such as America Reads, aimed at raising reading literacy among youth (Morrow & Woo, 2001). National programs—such as TRIO, Talent Search & GEAR UP—are long standing programs that provide pre-college students with support and address barriers that hinder student success. These programs aim at addressing barriers based on social, academic, and financial means for the benefit of the under-represented pre-college student (Domina, 2009). The programs are designed to specifically engage students, through making sure that under-represented students and pre-college students are able to have access to networks that help navigate the intricacies of applying for and going to college (Perna & Swail, 2001).

③ *Information-based outreach programs.*
A final section of pre-college-based outreach and one that is vital for the pre-college movement going forward is information-/learning-based outreach. Information- and learning-based outreach produces the most potential for each facet of a pre-college program to develop holistically throughout a community and within an institution of higher education. Often in information-/learning-based outreach, the objectives may not be directly linked to serving the pre-college student audience, but to provide a foundation for university students (undergraduate and graduate), faculty, and

staff to connect to pre-college students through service-learning opportunities, community engagement, and as part of research-based, broader impact programs.

Colleges and universities may choose to engage pre-college students within their labs as junior researchers or develop specific individualized programming offered during the summer in the form of a residential summer camp. Regardless of the activity, faculty and undergraduates have a vast opportunity to impact pre-college students as it relates to their institutional work. The Summer Academic and Youth Programs office within Bowling Green State University provides one example of how a university created efforts to increase pre-college programming by providing faculty support to develop outreach specifically for pre-college students around academic-major explorations, as a way of highlighting faculty research and recruiting new students to their field of study.

Regardless of outreach category, there are endless possibilities in which universities can strengthen and develop pre-college efforts through intentionally designing learning practices that tangentially support all aspects of university outreach.

University Examples and Resources

Need-Based Program
K8 – Tigers Program, Auburn University
College offices, especially admissions offices, are places that sometimes receive inquiries and requests from all audiences about how to obtain information or freebies (pennants, shirts, flyers) for school districts looking to make students aware of college opportunities. These requests come in

many forms, from elementary students learning to write formal letters to high school offices looking for college information for a college night. Unfortunately, these requests often fall through the cracks as admission offices are not designed to address such specific requests. Therefore, when a request came through to Auburn University's Center for Educational Outreach and Engagement to help out with one of these request anomalies, the challenge was met with an unprecedented return. What started as a small request of following up with a few schools turned into an initiative known as the K8 – Tigers Program. Within the first year the office corresponded with over 420 schools, sending college information and promotional items of various types all across the United States. What started as a small request within the community turned into a dynamic call to action for Auburn University's Center for Educational Outreach and Engagement who were able to fulfill the need, thus linking pre-college students with information and opportunity.

Awareness-Based Program
Vetward Bound Science Discovery Club
MSU College of Veterinary Medicine
For almost a decade the After-School Science Discovery Club, a smaller program within the Vetward Bound Program, offered science discovery opportunities for students in the local school district. University undergraduate students served as science club mentors and facilitated hands-on experiments from the science club curriculum throughout the academic year to seven afterschool programs ranging in grades 2nd through 12th. In years when grant funding and additional economic support was insufficient to support the science club undergraduates as student employees, the Vetward Bound Science Club program partnered with the Office of Service Learning and Civic

Engagement to provide placement sites for university undergraduate students needing service learning credit. In time—due to the dynamics of the science discovery club's focus, and the experience of working with a range of elementary and high school students surrounding reading, math, and science—a lasting partnership with providing service learning placements was created. Through this partnership the Science Discovery Club was able to subsidize student employment costs by filling the need with service learning placements, allowing the science club to double in size and offer fourteen clubs. Concurrently, the university undergraduate students were able to use the experience as their service learning credit required by most majors. In conclusion, one of the most exciting returns of investment the science discovery club was able to witness, is the subsequent hiring of science club mentors who were former science club participants in their elementary years.

Information/-Learning-Based Programs
Summer Academic Youth Programs

Increasing in popularity are K-12 science outreach related curriculums that are directly connected to institutional research. This in part is due to an on-going requirement established within funding agencies such as the National Science Foundation (NSF) that researchers must incorporate broader impacts into their work (Komoroske, Hameed, Szoboszlai, Newsom, & Williams, 2015). Therefore, researchers, in particular scientists, are starting to seek out partnerships within the K-12 pipeline to meet these goals.

Unfortunately, science educational outreach with the exception of broader impacts is undervalued within research and faculty settings overall (Komoroske et al., 2015). The institutional importance of research often places publications as the priority. Therefore, one direct opportunity for universities to engage in low risk pre-college programming would be to connect with faculty whose research requires broader impacts, by providing faculty an avenue to pursue research while incorporating programming for pre-college audiences, in which both the university and the student will benefit.

The Office of Summer Academic Youth Programming (SAYP) at Bowling Green State University works with departments across campus to assist in the creation of non-credit academic summer camps for pre-college students. These programs are linked to an academic major's university services or are part of broader impact initiatives within faculty research. Through the event management of the SAYP office, faculty and units interested in developing pre-college programs receive support from housing and logistics of campers on campus to complying with university policies and procedures. The SAYP office removes several of the common barriers that might interfere with initiatives related to developing pre-college programs at the university level.

Conclusion

As the audience makeup of institutions begins to change, and as pressure mounts with reports of rising tuition costs, universities need to embrace opportunities that develop pathways and strengthen relationships through offering pre-college outreach programs for K-12 students.

Universities have many options when it comes to creating these opportunities for pre-college outreach, such as developing programs that are need-based, awareness-based, or information-based to meet the needs of the community and the institution. In the beginning, there may be some obstacles to overcome, such as administration and logistics of hosting minors on campus or additional time needed for faculty to prepare appropriate pedagogy for teaching content to younger audiences. However, despite these initial obstacles, the ripple effect of universities engaging in pre-college outreach has the potential for lasting impacts that should not be ignored.

About the Author
Kari Storm earned her B.S. in Biological Sciences from Lyman Briggs College at Michigan State University. Following graduation, she served for eight years as outreach coordinator with the Vetward Bound Program through the Michigan State University College of Veterinary Medicine. In 2016, Kari transitioned to Bowling Green State University, where she now holds the position of summer academic and youth programs coordinator. With more than ten years dedicated to engaging with faculty, staff, and students, Kari enjoys creating experiences for all learners (teachers and students alike) involved with pre-college outreach.

REFERENCES

Astin, A. W., Sax, L. J., & Avalos, J. (1999). Long-term effects of volunteerism during the undergraduate years. *The Review of Higher Education, 22*(2), 187–202.

Blonshine, R. L. (2014*). Impact of mentoring on former pre-college program participants: Gaining while giving back.* (Order No. 3628121, University of Southern California). ProQuest Dissertations and Theses, 100. Retrieved from http://digitallibrary.usc.edu/cdm/ref/collection/p15799coll3/id/410857

Desiato, V. (2014, January 20). *Honoring Martin Luther King Jr: life's most persistent and urgent question.* Retrieved from https://blog.mass.gov/hhs/uncategorized/honoring-martin-luther-king-jr-lifes-most-persistent-and-urgent-question/

Domina, T. (2009). What works in college outreach: Assessing targeted and schoolwide interventions for disadvantaged students. *Educational Evaluation and Policy Analysis, 31*(2),127–152. doi:10.3102/ 0162373709333887

Grawe, N. D. (2018). *Demographics and the demand for higher education.* Baltimore, MD: Johns Hopkins University Press.

Jenkins, M. (2009). The effects of a pre-college program on at-risk students. *Research and Teaching in Developmental Education, 26*(1), 3–9.

Komoroske, L. M., Hameed, S. O., Szoboszlai, A. I., Newsom, A. J., & Williams, S. L. (2015). A scientist's guide to achieving broader impacts through K–12 STEM collaboration. *Bioscience, 65*(3), 313–322. doi:10.1093/biosci/biu222

Lockeman, K. S. (2012). *The impact of service-learning among other predictors for persistence and degree completion of undergraduate students* (Doctoral dissertation, Virginia Commonwealth University). Retrieved from https://scholarscompass.vcu.edu/etd/2910

Morrow, L. M. (Ed.), & Woo, D. G. (Ed.) (2001). *Tutoring programs for struggling readers: The America Reads Challenge.* Rutgers Invitational Symposia on Education. New York, NY: Guilford Publications. (ERIC Document Reproduction Service No. ED480246)

O'Dell, I., Smith, M. R., & Born, J. E. (2016). The effect of pre-college involvement on leadership efficacy, citizenship and social change behaviors among college students. *College Student Journal, 50*(1), 71–85.

Perna, L. W., & Swail, W. S. (2001). Pre-college outreach and early intervention. *Thought & Action, 17*(1), 99–110.

Thomas, L. (2011). Do pre-entry interventions such as 'Aimhigher' impact on student retention and success? A review of the literature. *Higher Education Quarterly, 65*(3), 230–250. doi:10.1111/j.1468-2273.2010.00481.x

Chapter 11

Pre-College Programs on Diversity in Higher Education

By Candy McCorkle, Ph.D.,
Western Michigan University

Ubuntu
"I see you therefore I am seen."

Introduction

It has long been the practice that the K-12 educational system has served as the pipeline for colleges and universities. However, we have not always explored how non-academic experiences specifically influence the student's experience in postsecondary educational settings. In this chapter, we will explore how experiences in secondary school focused on engaging with diverse cultural groups can shape the level of diversity and inclusion on college campuses. Pre-college programs have a unique opportunity to intentionally engage students in activities that expose them to cultures in which they are not members as well as to foster the development of their own cultural identity.

The Role of Pre-College Program Provision of Exposure to Diversity

With the pervasiveness of social media, students are exposed to a variety of ideas and people. A benefit of the social media phenomenon is that its anonymity allows people who may not typically interact with one another to engage in conversation or activity. Although social media allows for greater interaction with variety of people, those interactions are not intentionally targeted to shape cultural awareness. Pre-college programs' primary goal is to expose K-12 students to college and to assist them in becoming college ready. One of the skills imperative to navigating college successfully is being able to engage with people who are different than oneself. Students may attend secondary school with students from different backgrounds, but may not engage in meaningful ways with those different than they are. Pre-college programs can be intentional in creating programming that fosters cultural awareness and the exposure to cultural/social identities.

Before exposing students to people from different cultural/ social identities, it is important to understand the various attributes of diversity. Often when diversity is addressed, ethnicity and race are the first attributes considered. However, diversity is broad in its attributes. Some of the primary attributes which are considered cultural/social identities would be: race/ethnicity; gender identity; sexuality; socio-economic status; nationality; religion/spirituality; ideology; and ability (physical and psychological).

As individuals we all hold more than one cultural/social identity. These identities intersect, creating different experiences for us based on the saliency of each identity at a given moment. For example, race/ethnicity describes if a person identifies as Black/African-American, White, Latina/o, Native American, Asian American, Pacific Islander, etc. For individuals who identify as Black/African-American or Latina/o, race/ethnicity may be very a salient identity because of the historical marginalization and oppression experienced by these identity groups as a result of their race/ethnicity.

In addition to race/ethnicity, the cultural identity of ability (physical or psychological) is often shrouded in inaccuracies and stigmas. Research shows that "1-4 young people between the ages of 18–24 have a diagnosable mental illness" (Carnevale, Fasules, Quinn, & Pletier-Campbell, 2019). It is often believed that students with mental health issues are seen as not intellectually competent to attend and strive in college. So students who have a diagnosis or experience symptoms are less likely to address the issues due to the stigmas. Pre-college programs can assist with minimizing the stigma of mental illness by providing programming to educate students prior to entering college on the impact of mental health and resources to assist in addressing any concerns. Talking openly about mental health issues with students helps to normalize it and not make it a barrier to college.

In order to continue to break down the barriers for success in college, it is imperative to have students experience cultural dissonance or disequilibrium. The occurrence of cultural dissonance or disequilibrium is to purposely challenge a student's worldview and understanding of their cultural experiences. Students entering college will be exposed to others who have experienced the world differently. By creating cultural dissonance, students will begin to not place a value of good or bad or right or wrong on cultural experiences and instead will learn that they are just different. In order for students to recognize that there are different ways to experience the world, their existing worldview must be challenged. Examples of how a pre-college program can create disequilibrium is by bringing students to campus to engage with different groups. I hosted high school students from Detroit Public Schools and public charter schools in Detroit on the campus of Alma College for one week. The students were exposed to different types of foods, and students who looked, dressed, and sounded differently than they did. These students were also able to take two academic courses and attend several presentations on aspects of campus life. This one-week experience challenged the students' perceptions of school and normalcy. The students also spent the week reflecting on what their post-high school goals were, how college could assist them in reaching their goals, and how this experience impacted their view of college. At the conclusion of the week the students gave presentations on their responses to the aforementioned three questions. To further challenge the students who reside in a diverse urban city, the week was spent in a rural predominantly White community. The purpose of the program was to challenge the students' worldviews so that their perception of college was realistic.

In addition to shaping new worldviews for students, pre-college programs also challenge the students as well as the educational institutions to reframe the approach for assisting students. So often students are invited to participate in bridge programs because of some perceived or real deficit. In the field of education, we design programs to assist students labeled as "at-risk." Some of the risk factors we identify are low income, academic underprepared, first-generation, from a historically marginalized population, or having a disability. Pike, Hansen, and Childress (2014–2015) have found that being a member of a historically marginalized group increases the risk factors for students not attaining a degree without some form of intervention. This suggests that a pre-college program would be positively related to degree attainment. However, in the same article the authors found that individuals who have a sense of confidence are more likely to attain a four-year degree (Pike et al., 2014–2015). It is important to address the deficits students have in order to help them transition successfully to college but it is equally important to identify strengths. Pike et al. (2014-2015) found in their study that developing programs that focus on the strengths students possess allows them to cultivate a sense of confidence. By engaging in activities in which they are confident, students are more likely to experience success and demonstrate resilience.

One of the risk factors in which higher education is beginning to gain insight is first-generation students. The term first-generation is used frequently but its definition varies. In this text it refers to a student whose parents did not attend college or did not complete college (Bui, 2002; Lohfink & Paulsen, 2005; Ting, 1998). Attending college is significant for a first-generation student because unlike their second- and third-generation peers, these students have limited exposure to college and/or an uncertain expectation of college (Pike et al., 2014–2015). A pre-college program is essential for assisting these students in learning to successfully navigate the college landscape.

Creating a Diverse Pipeline to Higher Education
The students possessing one or more risk factor are the fastest growing demographic of college-eligible individuals (Montemurri & Tanner, 2014). A natural question might be: why these students want to go to college if statistically their chances of attaining a degree are poor? The risk factors are more significant when projecting four-year degree attainment; the statistics are not the same for students engaging in other postsecondary paths. Pre-college programs can assist students in learning what it means to go to college. Going to college is not just declaring a major, taking classes, and living in residence halls. Instead, going to college requires a student to develop skills: to live independently, manage their time, become financially literate, develop self-advocacy, and interact with others who are different.

Many students state they want to attend college in order to attain a good job that pays well. Some students want a particular career that requires a specific degree, while some parents expect for their student to have the experience of living away from home. In defining what going to college entails, it is important for students to consider the reasons they want to attend college because that becomes the initial motivation. Often not discussed are the types of postsecondary educational opportunities. Society historically emphasized that students attend four-year colleges but that is not the only option for postsecondary education. Pursuing a credit-bearing certificate or an associate degree is also considered "college." Cost is another factor for students to consider. Four-year institutions can be expensive so a two-year college may be more economical to start. Pre-college programs can assist students in learning about the options of paying for college and the real cost of attending college. The cost of college is both financial and social. The financial cost is easier to grasp by students but most do not expect to pay a social price. The social price is significant for students who have some of the aforementioned risk factors. Students from marginalized populations attending a predominantly White institution (PWI) may feel isolated, as if their experience is not valued and therefore they do not belong (Bui, 2002; Lohfink & Paulsen, 2005). This experience creates real challenges to developing relationships with classmates and instructors. By participating in a pre-college program, students can be exposed to the possible social costs and develop effective coping methods.

One means of minimizing the sense of isolation is to select a school based on fit. That fit can be measured by mission, affordability, student and faculty demographic, size, majors, and extra-curricular activities. In order to increase a student's

chances of success, it is imperative to assist them in selecting a school that fits their needs and ultimate goals.

Benefits of Diverse Student Populations to the College Experience

The demographics of college students will change significantly in the next 10–20 years and colleges need to be prepared now to recruit and retain these students (Montemurrie
& Tanner, 2014). As minority populations grow faster than
the White population our college campuses will begin to
change. Research suggests that students from minority
groups are more likely to possess at least two of the other
risk factors identified as inhibitors to degree attainment
(Pike et al., 2014–2015). Pre-college programs have a unique
ability to begin working with these students in K-12 to help
them develop the skills they will need to succeed in college.

Assisting minority students with other risk factors that
impact achievement in college is not the only reason to
promote postsecondary education for these students. It is
important to encourage these students to attend college
because of the social and academic benefits. Students who
exist in diverse communities are forced to learn about themselves in order to more effectively engage with those who
are different. These students also develop a solid sense of
their strengths and deficits. In addition to learning about
self, students have the opportunity to learn about those
who are different. The awareness of others can influence
the student to begin to value and appreciate differences.
As they continue to engage with individuals from different
cultures, religions, genders, sexual orientation, abilities, and
political ideologies, an appreciation for diverse perspectives
begins to take shape. The minority students as well as their
White counterparts experience more challenges, which
strengthens their learning and acquisition of knowledge

(Lohfink & Paulsen, 2005). These students learn to be better problem solvers because they are able to use multiple perspectives to inform their decisions. By crossing the proverbial culture aisle, these students are more adept at navigating a variety of social situations which can assist in lowering the social cost of college (Lohfink & Paulsen, 2005; Pike et al., 2014-2015). Pre-college programs assist by identifying these students early and working with them to assist in diversifying higher education with students who are equipped to address the challenges of college.

Personal Reflection
As a first-generation, African-American, cisgender female from a low socioeconomic background, I did not fit the mode for the ideal prospective college student. I did possess an anomaly, in that I had strong grades, high test scores, and a cadre of Advanced Placement courses. The academic expectations of college were not the deterrent for me—it was the social expectations that were my challenge. As I reflect back on how I got to college, it was the science and math pre-college programs I participated in that made the difference in me feeling as if I could become a college student and actively engage in the campus culture. These programs are imperative for preparing students who have the ability to succeed in college but are without the proper training and coaching. The earlier programs can begin to work with students, the greater the odds increase for them to attain a college degree (Pike et al., 2014-2015). It is important that we create a postsecondary-education-going culture regardless of what type of postsecondary education is sought. We begin to shape this culture by engaging students in programs such as Upward Bound, GEAR UP, TRIO, and other programs that introduce K–12 students to the possibilities after high school. If we can control for the risk factors by creating more programs that make access and

attainment equitable, we will change the demographic of colleges and universities not just by ethnicity and/or race, gender or abilities, but by enrolling students who are better prepared. This will assist higher education to truly become an inclusive environment.

There is a wonderful African concept called "Ubuntu," which loosely translates in English as "I see you therefore I am seen." If we begin to see our students for the strengths they possess and the contributions they can make to our organizations, they will begin to see the value of a college education beyond just a degree and a job, but as a means of improving the quality of life for all. Pre-college programs can play an important role in planting the seeds for a diverse student population.

About the Author

Dr. Candy McCorkle currently serves as the Vice President of Diversity and Inclusion at Western Michigan University in Kalamazoo, Michigan. Prior to joining the senior adminis-tration of WMU, she served as the Assistant Vice President of Student Affairs and the Director of Diversity and Inclusion at Alma College in Alma, Michigan. She has served in higher education for over 20 years beginning her career as an Asso-ciate Professor of Psychology at Spring Arbor University in Spring Arbor, Michigan. She also served as the director of the Master's of Counseling program at Spring Arbor Uni-versity and was an Assistant Professor of Counseling and Director of the Global Campus Counseling program at Central Michigan University in Mt. Pleasant, Michigan. Prior to serving at Alma College, Dr. McCorkle served as the Adjunct Administrator and Assistant Dean of the Honors program at Jackson College, Jackson, MI. She has also taught at the Moscow Christian School of Psychology,

Moscow, Russia. She earned her B.A. in Psychology at Wright State University in Dayton, Ohio; her M.S. in Clinical Psychology from Eastern Michigan University in Ypsilanti, Michigan; and her Ph.D. in Counselor Education and Supervision from Western Michigan University in Kalamazoo, Michigan. As an administrator, educator, and counselor, Dr. McCorkle has always demonstrated her commitment to moving organizations toward inclusivity.

REFERENCES

Bui, K. (2002). First-generation college students at four-year university: Background characteristics, reasons for pursing higher education, and first-year experiences. *College Student Journal, 31*(1), 3–11.

Carnevale, A. P., Fasules, M. L., Quinn, M. C., & Peltier-Campbell, K. (2019). Born to win, schooled to lose: Why equally talented students don't get equal chances to be all they can be. *Georgetown University Center on Education and the Workforce, McCourt School of Public Policy*, 1–51.

Lohfink, M. M., & Paulsen, M. B. (2005). Comparing the determinants of persistence for first generation and continuing-generation students. *Journal of College Student Development, 46*(4), 409–428.

Montemurri, P., & Tanner, K. (2014, Oct. 22). By 2060, a much more multi-cultural Michigan will emerge. *Detroit Free Press*. https://www.freep.com/story/news/local/michigan/2014/10/24/michigan-diversity-index-racial-demographics/17671861/

Pike, G. R., Hansen, M. J., & Childress, J. E. (2014–2015). The influence of students' pre-college characteristics, high school experiences, college expectations, and initial enrollment characteristics on degree attainment. *Journal of College Student Retention, 16*(1), 1–23.

Ting, S-M. (1998, Winter). Predicting first-year grades and academic progress of college students of first-generation and low-income families. *Journal of College Admissions, 158*, 14–23.

Chapter 12

Program Showcase:
Queer Academics and Activism—
A Program at Brandeis University

By Lisa DeBenedictis, Brandeis University

Editors' Notes:
As this book was being assembled, this new pre-college program was launching. We wanted to showcase it as part of our writings about diversity and inclusion.

About Brandeis University

Brandeis University was founded in 1948 by the American Jewish community at a time when Jews and other ethnic and racial minorities, and women, faced discrimination in higher education. Brandeis' visionary founders established a nonsectarian research university that welcomed talented faculty and students of all beliefs. Named after Louis D. Brandeis, former United States Supreme Court Justice, the university reflects his dedication to open inquiry and the pursuit of truth, insistence on critical thinking, and his commitment to helping common people. With social justice central to the Brandeis mission, the university embraces diversity and inclusivity, striving to reflect the heterogeneity of the United States and the world community whose ideas and concerns it shares.

About The Rabb School and Precollege Programs Office

Located in Waltham, Massachusetts, Brandeis today is a mid-size, top tier, research university with global reach, attracting students and faculty from around the world to pursue learning and scholarship at the highest levels. In addition to its founding focus on the undergraduate School of Arts and Sciences, Brandeis schools today also include the Graduate School of Arts and Sciences, Heller School for Social Policy and Management, Brandeis International Business School, and the Rabb School of Continuing Studies. Among these schools, the Rabb School of Continuing Studies welcomes a diverse range of students, from retired individuals to working professionals to high school students, and is home to the Brandeis Office of Precollege Programs.

For over a decade, Brandeis has offered outstanding educational experiences for high school students from throughout the United States and the world, in areas including the arts, sciences, humanities, and service learning through programs such as: Genesis: Jewish Leadership Program (established through a generous grant from Steven Spielberg's Righteous Persons Foundation); BIMA: Jewish Arts; the Global Youth Summit on the Future of Medicine; App Design; Service Corps; and new for 2019, the Queer Academics and Activism Program.

**Queer Academics and Activism Program –
Introduction, Origin, and Need**
Queer Academics and Activism: A Seminar on LGBTQIA+ Histories and Futures—also known as the QAA Program— is a new and timely addition to the Brandeis program offerings for high school students and is the first-of-its-kind in the nation program. A joint initiative of Brandeis Precollege Programs and the Women's, Gender, and Sexuality Studies Program at Brandeis, this program is designed with the collaborative programmatic and academic strengths and resources of both departments and strongly aligns with the Brandeis mission and foundation of social justice and inclusivity.

The idea for QAA began to develop about five years ago. Students participating in, or exploring, the *Gender, Sexuality and Society* course offered through the Brandeis Genesis program expressed interest in a program fully dedicated to the inquiry of gender identity and sexual orientation outside of the Jewish leadership context Genesis provides. At the same time, across Precollege Programs, staff increasingly worked with teens of varying gender identities and sexual orientations, finding that in many areas, LGBTQIA+ identifying high school students and allies are often underserved or marginalized within their schools and communities.

The Director of the Office of Precollege Programs at the time was in conversation with the Chair of the Women's, Gender, and Sexuality Studies Program at Brandeis about these issues. That program had a strong history as a locus of research, education, social engagement, and activities that explore and expand our collective understanding of how gender and sexuality intersect with race, class, culture, religion, ability, and more. Offering both undergraduate and graduate degree programs, the Women's, Gender, and Sexuality Studies Program was the ideal collaborator and thought partner with Precollege Programs, bringing together Precollege's history of offering exceptional residential programs for high school students and the Women's, Gender, and Sexuality Studies Program's expertise on academic content as well as language and best practices specific to designing QAA, and also relevant to all high school programs offered through Precollege. Conversations evolved and the leadership of each group decided to pilot the QAA program in the summer of 2019. They began to work, in detail, on the curriculum in the summer of 2018 and built out the program over the next academic year.

Queer Academics and Activism Program – Overview, Purpose, and Goals

Queer Academics and Activism (QAA) is a six-day residential summer program offered for rising 10th, 11th, and 12th grade students with demonstrated commitment to and interest in LGBTQIA+ issues as well as strong academic records. Students apply for the program and, in some cases, are nominated by teachers, school counselors, LGBTQIA+ and ally organizations, or other adults within their communities.

The structure and scope of QAA differentiate this program from others offered for LGBTQIA+ teens. Designed for both LGBTQIA+ teens and allies, QAA goes beyond identity formation and community building and applies an academic lens to the queer experience to help queer youth and allies better know their histories and consider their futures. Students explore queer issues related to the arts, health, education, and religion and participate in daily lectures and discussion groups led by Brandeis undergraduate and graduate level faculty who are experts in these fields. Faculty lectures are complemented by field trips and supplemental activities, as well as small group discussions led by faculty mentors who will serve as part of the program staff team and help to frame and further the faculty lectures. In addition, faculty mentors will help QAA participants in conducting their own research and developing their final projects that they present at the program's conclusion and may take back with them to implement in their home communities.

At the center of this effort is the idea that many LGBTQIA+ teens and their allies do not know the history of related efforts and this lack of historical understanding may limit the changes they wish to be and make in the world. The goal of this program is not to train activists, but to teach young people, who may become leaders of social change efforts in these areas, about their history so they can build on what took place in the past and further develop these efforts moving forward.

**Queer Academics and Activism Program –
Student Life and Support**
In addition to the academic focus of the QAA Program, student life is an important aspect, as the program is residential and participants will have the opportunity to experience life on a college campus. As with all programs offered through the Precollege Programs Office, QAA students will get the chance to learn in Brandeis classrooms and lecture halls, eat in the campus dining hall, live in the residence halls, and enjoy the many indoor and outdoor community spaces of the 235-acre Brandeis campus. For QAA, participants will be housed in single rooms, with a shared bathroom facility, and communal living space. Building community is integral to each pre-college program, and this aspect is especially important for the queer teens and allies who participate in QAA and are seeking to expand their network of peers and mentors.

Faculty mentor and residential advisor QAA Program staff positions are open to all eligible internal and external applicants. Brandeis undergraduates, graduate students, and alumni who have studied with the Women's, Gender, and Sexuality Studies Program are valuable resources in recruiting the staff team for QAA, as ideally staff will be adept in both discussing and teaching queer issues, likely through a combination of academic major and personal or professional experience, and also serve as positive models of Brandeis community members. In this regard, being role models that the QAA students may view as a resource as they think about potential academic majors and choices for college and beyond, the Brandeis Women's, Gender, and Sexuality Studies Program undergraduates, graduate students, and alumni will help to illustrate academic pathways for the high school students and provide a connection to the broader Brandeis community. The faculty are drawn, to the extent possible, from faculty currently affiliated with the Brandeis Women's, Gender, and Sexuality Studies Program, giving high school students access to some of the national thought leaders on these issues.

As with all programs offered through Precollege, QAA staff will attend a multi-day training prior to QAA students' arrival on campus. This training will cover aspects including: policies and procedures related to working with and supporting the physical and emotional well-being of teens in a residential environment, Precollege and Brandeis rules and community expectations, and considerations in working with queer teens. The expertise of the Women's, Gender, and Sexuality Studies Program surrounding language, definitions, pronouns, living spaces, and best practices is valuable in designing QAA staff training, and helpful in refining these aspects as they relate to supporting the teens who participate in all Brandeis Precollege Programs.

Supporting the QAA Program is also the QAA Advisory Board, a seven-member committee in this first year. Ranging in age, academic and professional background, and geographic location, the Advisory Board has worked closely with the Precollege Programs and Women's, Gender, and Sexuality Studies Program team to provide feedback, resources, and introductions in areas such as curricular content and program structure, outreach, and fundraising. In this first year, the QAA Program is fortunate to have supporters, external and internal, who have provided funding for scholarships for students to attend as well as other forms of support. In addition to individual campus partners who share enthusiasm for and interest in QAA, the Brandeis Pride Alliance has offered assistance in attending the student final presentations, chaperoning field trips and events, and broadly helping to foster a welcoming introduction to the campus community for QAA students. Precollege Programs and the Women's, Gender, and Sexuality Studies Program are thankful for the external and internal partners' support and, in regard to scholarships, plan to continue to raise funds for future iterations of QAA so that this program, and all Precollege Programs, may be accessible to students regardless of their families' financial situation and circumstances.

In this first pilot year of QAA, roughly 20+ students are anticipated to attend, with the intention of expanding and strengthening the program next year and beyond. The program is structured so that each year may welcome new students as well as students returning for a subsequent year who will be introduced to fresh content. The QAA Program team has been impressed by the student applications received, representing a diversity of identities and orientations as well as geographic locations throughout the United States and abroad. The personal narratives shared in these applications—some of which are noted (and edited to respect anonymity) as excerpts below—have reinforced the need for this program and value it will contribute to students' lives:

Asexuality, which I identify as, is not well-known. I almost cried the first time I found an asexual character in a book... she was proof that my identity was something other people had felt before. I wasn't an anomaly. I want to use my experience to help others find that validation.

The experience of going to school in a predominantly homophobic town and school system and spending the past few years trying to make improvements has given me a unique background. When I was in 7th grade, a middle school Gay Straight Alliance (GSA) started...By 8th grade I became the president of the GSA and got to experience firsthand the difficulties that came with. From posters constantly getting vandalized or ripped down, administration doing little to support us out of fear of complaints from homophobic parents, and the confidentiality of LGBTQ+ students breached when people decided to go to the meetings as a joke and then out members to the school.

I think living in [my home community] will give me a unique perspective. I don't have a good frame of reference for what other queer people experience but [my hometown community] is not ideal. I love my school and the opportunities I have access to...but there is always fear of being judged by my classmates and fear of being assaulted in public...

I know [my home state] doesn't sound like it holds much diversity, and frankly that's because it doesn't. It holds... outdated laws, and old prejudices. But it also holds good people. It holds gay people, closeted people, people who speak so loud that sometimes I forget they are not supposed to speak. My dream is to be one of these people; someone who speaks loud enough that it feels like the state is finally listening...I think maybe I could take the things I learn in this program back [home], and that maybe then it would feel like everything hard here has been worth it. I think the LGBTQ+ kids here need proof that our stories mean something. Because they do.

Part 2: Post Program—Afterthoughts

The Queer Academics and Activism Program (QAA) successfully ran for a week in June 2019, and exceeded student, staff, and faculty expectations in many ways. Twenty-three students attended, representing 11 states including California, Connecticut, Indiana, Massachusetts, North Carolina, New Hampshire, New Jersey, New York, Oregon, Virginia, and Texas. The program also included an international student from Mexico. Rising sophomores, juniors, and seniors in high school were all represented within the cohort. Many participants identified as members of the LGBTQIA+ community and the program included allies as well.

After an application and interview process, three residential staff were selected to provide day-to-day supervision in the residence hall, on-campus, and during off-campus outings, with a goal to create a welcoming, student life experience, and to provide mentorship to the QAA students. Residential staff included a Brandeis undergraduate student within the Women's, Gender, and Sexuality Studies Program, an alum of the undergraduate program, and a graduate student within the Women's, Gender, and Sexuality Studies Program who was also the program assistant and social media lead for QAA. The alum and program assistant also served as faculty mentors for the program, helping to integrate themes presented in faculty lectures, discussions, and outings into a holistic experience. The faculty mentors also guided the students in their individual final project presentations of their own choosing and design through a combination of discussions, lesson plans, and research at the Brandeis library.

Upon checking in for the program, participants received an internally designed program guidebook for their use and reference throughout the week. This guidebook included the program schedule, staff and faculty profiles, welcome letters from program and university leadership, information on field trips, and the lesson plans and assignments for both the daily faculty lecture discussions and the culminating project and presentation. Learning goals outlined for the program included providing students with the ability to:

- Describe the evolution of terms and identity concepts in the LGBTQIA+ communities and explain some of the factors that influenced changes over time.
- Define intersectionality and demonstrate through example what it means to use an intersectional perspective to understand queer history.
- Provide a brief overview of LGBTQIA+ activism in the United States and offer examples of the effects of that history on the present as related to health, education, religion, and/or art.
- Engage with their own communities around LGBTQIA+ issues and ground their queer activist work in more historical and comprehensive context.

Students achieved these goals through their daily lectures and discussions led by Brandeis faculty and dedicated project preparation time led by faculty mentors. The program included two field trips in Boston, spanning both health and visual and performing arts, that likewise had an LGBTQIA+ focus and complemented the academic learning.

On the final day of the program, the students presented their final projects spanning a variety of issues that impact the LGBTQIA+ community within North America, and presented their work in an event that was open to the Brandeis community and to the public. Attendees included: program staff and faculty; university-wide students, staff, and faculty;

_____

family of the participants; advisory board members; and supporters and friends of the program. Following the poster and presentation session, a closing ceremony was held where students were recognized for their work and participation in the program and received certificates of completion.

Toward the conclusion of the program, staff gathered feedback from participants on various aspects of the academic, residential, and overall program experience. Many noted the lectures and field trips as highlights of the experience, as well as the opportunity to meet and connect with a community of peers from throughout North America, and especially commented that the program structure and staff created a safe supportive community. Some verbally conveyed to staff that the program was "the best week of their life" and many expressed an interest in returning to participate in QAA for a subsequent summer. For suggestions, some students shared that they would like the program to be longer. Others expressed an interest in more free time and a later curfew.

Reflecting on the program, students and staff overwhelmingly shared that the QAA Program had a positive impact on them. Excerpts of their reflections, originally shared in a July 3, 2019 BrandeisNOW article featuring QAA and titled *High Schoolers Converge at Brandeis for First-of-Its-Kind LGBTQIA+ Academic Program* (brandeis.edu/now/2019/july/qaa-precollege-program.html) are noted below:

I've been totally blown away by the questions they ask in lectures and the passion they have. They've come together and shared their experiences and I'm immensely proud and feel very inspired...
(Sierra Dana, Brandeis Class of 2020, QAA Residential Advisor)

It's interesting to be here, because as a queer person I've never had the experience of sitting down in a formal place and have someone go over the history of these issues. I've never met people who do queer studies professionally – all I had known previously was what I learned on my own or from people my age. To see how older people approach this, as adults, is really useful. I also consider myself an activist in my hometown, so what I've learned here is really useful for me to bring back, so I appreciate that.
(Evelyn Bernstein, rising senior from Monmouth County, New Jersey, QAA Participant)

I didn't expect to see students from so many parts of the U.S., or even outside of it, just maybe a bunch of people from Boston and New York, but that's not the case and it's really exciting. It's interesting to hear what they deal with locally, and I've also never thought of queer studies from a scholarly point of view. So I appreciate the new perspective. It's a lot better to learn it here than, say, on YouTube, because I'm surrounded by people who are qualified to speak about it and experienced in the field.
(Charlie Apple, rising sophomore from Corpus Christi, Texas, QAA Participant)

I am an ally, but I was worried before I came that I'd be an outsider in the community. I didn't want to be seen as an intruder, but I've been able to get to know this community that's been here throughout history. There are lessons here

that you don't get at school, which I think is one of the most impressive things about this program.
(Andrea Torres-Everest, rising senior from Monterrey, Mexico, QAA Participant)

About the Author
Lisa DeBenedictis is Program Director in the Office of Pre-college Programs at Brandeis University, where she oversees the educational, co-curricular, and residential experience for three precollege programs. Lisa has an A.B. from Harvard College and an Ed.M. from the Harvard Graduate School of Education.

Chapter 13

Importance of Research in Pre-College Programming

By Erika Carr, Ph.D., Kelly Schultz, Ph.D., and
Luke Steinman, Western Michigan University

Why is Research on Pre-college Programs and Outreach Important?

The role of pre-college programs in college recruitment and retention is a newer construct in higher education. Only recently have colleges and universities begun to utilize existing pre-college programs as a tool in their recruitment efforts. As pre-college programs have grown in value, there have been questions about their effectiveness. At this time, there is limited research on the effectiveness of pre-college programs and on pre-college programs in general. This chapter reviews the available literature and research on pre-college programs, but this new and growing field requires additional research, especially as it relates to pre-college programs' role in transitioning students to higher education.

Current Research Review

Impact of Pre-College Programs on College Attendance and Degree Attainment

There has been some research on the impact of pre-college programs as it relates to the programs' ability to positively influence college attendance and degree attainment.

Mattson (2007) examined which pre-college variables predicted college grade point average (GPA) for at-risk students. Three variables were found to be significant predictors to academic success: high school GPA, gender, and leadership experience. Since pre-college programs often provide services that increase high school GPA (tutoring, mentoring, etc.) as well as leadership experiences, this article connects pre-college programs to greater college attendance and degree attainment. Mattson (2007) pointed to controversy within the literature regarding the validity of SAT scores, and this study itself found it was not a predictor. As a result of the study's findings, Mattson (2007) recommended that higher education administrators re-evaluate the magnitude of pre-college variables, especially when deciding which students to admit and/or which are considered for academic support programs. The article also challenged higher education to not overemphasize SAT scores and questioned the current emphasis on college admissions tests.

Perna and Swail (2001) reviewed some of the early federally-funded college access intervention programs. They detailed some success with first-generation, low-income students gaining access to higher education through these programs, but also advocate for more funding to grow the programs. Perna and Swail (2001) argued that historically the government has relied on financial aid as a means of increasing college access, but a review of relevant research indicates this is not sufficient in creating opportunities for all students:

"the fact that gaps in access and completion have not been closed despite the resources the federal government has dedicated to closing them – suggests that merely making financial aid available for students to attend college is not enough to ensure that all students

have equal access to the benefits associated with earning a college degree." (Perna & Swail, 2001, p. 100).

Perna and Swail also reviewed the federal pre-college programs including Talent Search, GEAR UP, and Upward Bound, and indicated they have had an impact on students' access to higher education. Previously, using data from the National Educational Longitudinal Study (NELS), Horn and Chen (1998) showed that "moderate- to high-risk students who participated in high school outreach programs had almost double the odds of enrolling in a four-year college than their peers who did not participate" (p. 27). Perna and Swail (2001) argued that these pre-college programs, though often underfunded, have demonstrated an ability to increase college enrollment and degree attainment. However, Perna and Swail (2001) emphasized the importance of more research being needed to determine the effectiveness of pre-college programs.

Another researcher, Clasen (2006), examined the effectiveness of a specific pre-college program, Project STREAM. Clasen found that there was a strong, positive correlation between academic outcomes and participation in pre-college programs overall. In addition, the Pre-College Programs Report written by the American Association of Collegiate Registrars and Admissions Officers (AACRAO, 2018) found that 70% of those colleges surveyed either strongly agreed or somewhat agreed that pre-college programs are an important part of the enrollment pipeline at their institution. It is clear that higher education is recognizing the important role that pre-college programs have in increasing both college enrollment and retention.

Assessing the Experience of Pre-College Students

An area of interest to pre-college program researchers is how programs are experienced by the youth participating in them, including if the programs influence their knowledge and perceptions of postsecondary education, thereby increasing college access and success. Several studies discussed specific programs and their success rates with a college-going culture, but only a few articles examined the effects of students' pre-college experience or a systematic study of what attributes ensure a successful program. Two of those studies are described in this section.

A study by Terence Hicks, a professor at East Tennessee State University, "Assessing the Academic, Personal and Social Experiences of Pre-college Students" (Hicks, 2005) examined the pre- and post-participation effects of tran-sitional summer programs. Specifically, the study looked at pre-college students' perceptions, expectations, emotions, and knowledge about college. A total of 197 participants participated in either of two six-week summer programs: 1) Louis Stokes Alliance for Minority Participation Program (LSAMP), a program for traditional, first-time freshmen with outstanding performance in science and math in high school; or 2) the Preparation and Adjustment for College Entrance Program (PACE), a program for first-time, pre-college fresh-men, who had applied for full-time admission to the univer-sity but did not demonstrate all the criteria required due to deficiencies in their high school achievement. The students were given a pre- and post-participation questionnaire administered during the first and last weeks of the camps to measure Perceptions, Expectations, Emotions, and Knowl-edge (PEEK). PEEK, developed by Weinstein, Palmer, and Hanson (1995, cited in Hicks, 2005), was designed to elicit the thoughts that pre-college students had about their college expectations. A focus group with 15 students (10 from PACE and five from LSAMP) also took place. The study found the programs helped facilitate students' transition and adjustment to college life and improved persistence rates. Although the study highlighted the benefit of both programs, its results did reveal more impact for pre-college participants who were considered "at risk" by the institution. "Although it may be a good idea for all students, the structured summer program approach is particularly helpful for students considered at risk in a university setting" (Hicks, 2005, p. 24).

Another set of papers examines the results of a survey administered to many different types of pre-college programs by The College Board, in association with The Education Resources Institute (TERI) and the Council for Opportunity in Education (COE) in 1999. In the chapter, "Pre-College Outreach Programs: A National Perspective" in the book *Increasing Access to College: Extending Possibilities for All Students*, Swail and Perna (2002) describe in detail the federal programs dedicated to pre-college youth, while other programs are briefly described. The chapter spends the majority of its time analyzing the results of the survey, which asked respondents about financial support, program location, program goals and services, working with parents, program operation, targeting students, incentives for students, program staffing and training, and program implications. The researchers concluded that pre-college programs need to incorporate the following essential elements of successful outreach endeavors: a clear, focused mission and vision; early start; student motivation; parental involvement; collaboration; sustainable funding; practice of professionalism and personal development; a reliance on proven practices; standardized processes; and utilization of technology (Swail & Perna, 2002, pp. 30–31). Another conclusion from the study came from Perna and Swail (2001), who advocated that intervention programs begin earlier in the pre-college student's life and feel the programs are best served by focusing on those students who are academically able to be successful in college.

Review of Individual Pre-College Programs

In assessing the effectiveness of pre-college outreach programs, it is important to examine some of the federally funded TRIO programs used across the nation and understand the factors that lead to their success and outcomes. Since TRIO's creation through the Economic Opportunity Act of 1964 and Higher Education Act of 1965, programs like Upward Bound, Gaining Early Awareness and Readiness for Undergraduate Programs (GEAR UP), and Talent Search have been assisting students with preparation for higher education to find success in college and beyond. "The purpose of TRIO programs is to provide low-income and first-generation collegians with the skills, tools, and motivation integral to future educational successes" (U.S. Department of Education, "Gaining early awareness," n.d.) [Quinn 2015]. Programs like Upward Bound and GEAR UP were developed to help economically disadvantaged/lower SES students, along with first generation students, to complete their secondary education studies and find success in postsecondary institutions. Talent Search, on the other hand, provides opportunities for several age groups to develop leadership and scholarly potential for success in higher education.

In assessing the best practices from this broad array of programs, Gullatt and Jan (2003) found ten traits that all pre-college programs should embody if they hope to find success. These principles are: high standards for program students and staff, personalized attention for students, adult role models, peer support, K-12 program integration, strategically timed interventions, long-term investment in students, school/society bridge for students, scholarship assistance, evaluation designs that contribute results to interventions (Gullatt & Jan, 2003). Most programs focus on either informational outreach, career-based outreach, or academic support, but programs should strive to integrate components of all three into the services they provide (Gullatt & Jan, 2003).

The Upward Bound (UB) program began as a part of the Economic Opportunity Act and the Higher Education act of 1965. The program works to help first-generation college students from low-income families prepare for and enroll in institutions of higher education and provides continuous services throughout their secondary education. Upward Bound programs select a small group of students who meet their criteria for admission (first-generation college student and/or low-income). UB seeks to increase high school graduation rates, postsecondary enrollment, and baccalaureate degree attainment for this population as a whole (Partridge, 2016). Services include: weekly tutoring, math and science training, weekend Saturday academies focused on various aspects of college readiness/preparation and financial literacy, and a six-week supplemental summer component, during which students take classes, live on the college campus, and participate in career development activities. Through its efforts, Upward Bound has been found to increase high school graduation, college enrollment, college retention, and college graduation (Seftor, Mamun, & Schirm, 2009).

Talent Search, the second program created from the 1965 Economic Opportunity Act, works to "identify and assist

individuals from disadvantaged backgrounds who have potential to succeed in higher education" (U.S. Department of
Education, "Talent search program," n.d.). Through academic,
career, and financial counseling and support, Talent Search
helps to guide both active high school students and students
who have left secondary and postsecondary institutions
with hopes of postsecondary completion (U.S. Department
of Education, 2019). Talent Search participants have been
found to enroll in four-year colleges at a higher rate than
their peers who also qualified for the Talent Search program
(Brewer & McMahan Landers, 2005).

GEAR UP was developed in 1998 to help further expand the
reach of academic preparation and college readiness for low
income and/or first-generation students. Using a cohort-
based model, GEAR UP works with an entire grade of
students starting in their seventh grade year and provides
them continuous services through their twelfth grade
year—and in some programs, through their first year of
postsecondary studies (U.S. Department of Education,
"Gaining early awareness," n.d.). Through early introduction
to career exploration, college exposure through visits, tutoring and mentoring, summer camps, and financial assistance,
GEAR UP raises awareness and preparation for college
while helping students find their own pathways to success
(Standing, Judkins, Keller, & Shimshak, 2008). While GEAR
UP's impact has been found to be modest in participants'
middle and high school success, long term, postsecondary
outcomes are difficult to evaluate and have been limited
(Venezia & Jaeger, 2013).

Pre-College Program Data Review

Pre-College Programs Report

The American Association of Collegiate Registrars and Admissions Officers (AACRAO) completed a Pre-College Programs Report in 2018. The information was collected via a process termed as one of that month's "60-Second Surveys." For the purpose of this report, pre-college programming was defined as "university sponsored/organized programs and activities for K-12 school participants typically not yet enrolled in college as degree-seeking students" (AACRAO, 2018, p. 1). A pre-college programming unit was defined as "the university department and/or umbrella entity with responsibility for overall oversight of all pre-college programs at one college or university" (AACRAO, 2018, p. 1). They received responses from 451 different institutions of diverse sizes, types, and countries of origin. The survey focused on how pre-college programs on college campuses were structured and organized. In particular, the survey revealed how pre-college programs in higher education have been growing: "Most institutions (82%) report having pre-college programs" (AACRAO, 2018, p. 1) and, "Almost half of the institutions have increased the number of pre-college programs in the last three years" (AACRAO, 2018, p. 1). The survey also found that pre-college programs were most commonly administered by academic affairs, but that it was not uncommon for pre-college programs to exist in more than one institutional division. In addition to organization structure, the survey also examined perception of pre-college programs and found that 70% either strongly agree or somewhat agree that pre-college programs are an important part of the enrollment pipeline at their institution (AACRAO, 2018, p. 1). Community outreach, academic program exposure, and access to college top the list of the primary purpose of pre-college programs indicated by the survey. This study on pre-college programs and how they are both structured and perceived within higher education was an excellent start.

Pre-College Programming Model

In assessing the strength and weaknesses of pre-college offices across the nation, Sheth and Tremblay (2018) surveyed 14 pre-college programs on their views and outcomes regarding the 25 dimensions drawn from their research on and experience with best practices for pre-college programming. The 25 dimensions noted by Sheth and Tremblay (2018) are described in Chapter 5.

Of the dimensions assessed, the three most commonly noted as most important to pre-college programming and their outcomes are access and inclusion, compliance, and student engagement (Sheth & Tremblay, 2018). These dimensions are seen as pillars of consistent and successful pre-college programs across the United States and serve as the foundation for programs to build on. The study additionally identified the most important dimensions that were commonly missing from programs as "compliance, evaluation and assessment, and reporting"; however, the scores indicated the greatest weakness in "research, publishing and presenting; outcomes driven; and comprehensive" (Sheth & Tremblay, 2018, p. 17).

Blueprint for Success

The purpose of the paper "Blueprint for Success: Case Studies of Successful College Outreach Programs" (Swail, Quinn, Landis, & Fung, 2012) was to identify eight pre-college programs that showed excellent outcomes. They

---

measured academic improvement, high school completion, admission to college, and completion rate in college. They removed from consideration federal programs (like TRIO) and focused on community-based programs. They wished to add to the conversation on "best practices" in education by finding practices that work in pre-college programs. In the end, ten programs were studied to find common themes that could be generalized.

A good pre-college program must be intentional; it should have a clear mission and goals that have been generated by a thorough review of the community and the people involved. College attendance and completion must be expected of all students in the program and this should be communicated often and forcefully to the students and their parents. Considerable time must be devoted to collecting and using data to inform practices. Program management should be continuous and often; the program should constantly check itself against its goals and mission. Work with students should be intrusive; the staff in the programs should know their students and help them focus to attain their goals. As in many areas of life, the expectations for these students should be high and focused on academic development. Too often pre-college programs have to compete for funds, so successful programs are sustainable financially and have diverse monetary backing (Swail et al., 2012). The authors asked staff about the lessons learned while running their programs. Many want to create a program that is replicable and scalable, as they started small and grew to include multiple sites. They also indicated that planning and staffing are very important and time must be carved out to make sure that staff are focused on the mission and don't take on more than they can handle. The programs emphasized that data collection is important and must be intentionally built into the program. Without data, the program is less sustainable. Other important areas to consider are ensuring that students are career ready, that there is a college counselor on staff, and that programs run year-round. Finally, the authors listed the seven elements of an effective program which included: focus on strong leadership, set clear goals, build a cohesive community, document everything, be flexible, keep current in technology, and focus on the competition.

Future Research Directions

Gaps in Research

Despite a growing body of literature suggesting growth and success in student development and college persistence tied to federal TRIO programs, the existing research is limited. While little is known about the outcomes and effectiveness of federal TRIO programs, even less is known about the "thousands of other programs currently operating across the nation" (Swail & Perna, 2002, p. 17). Furthermore, research must pay mind to the role which expectations and outside perceptions play in grades earned and student retention when examining success in higher education (Hicks, 2005).

Next Steps in Pre-College Research

As well as filling the gaps in the research noted earlier, there is much more research that must be completed to truly determine the effectiveness of pre-college programs and their impact in college enrollment and degree attainment. Research on which specific services and program qualities ensure program success is essential. There is much data from the federal TRIO programs that could be analyzed or used to conduct a longitudinal study relating to college

---

access and attainment, and additional research on pre-college programs and how they operate within postsecondary education should be conducted. Finally, researchers should build on the work of Sheth and Tremblay (2018) in studying the 25 dimensions of offices of pre-college programs. The field of pre-college is so new, focusing on almost any area in the domain will lead to important contributions in the knowledge base.

About the Authors

Dr. Erika Carr, Director of Western Michigan University's Office of Pre-College Programming, is a first-generation college graduate, has 19 years of pre-college experience, directly supervises four pre-college programs, and teaches courses at WMU. She holds a Ph.D. in Higher Education Leadership and an M.A. in Counseling in Higher Education.

Dr. Kelly Schultz, Associate Director in the Office of Pre-College Programming at WMU, holds a Ph.D. in mathematics and an M.A. in Educational Leadership. For the past 11 years she has led the Academically Talented Youth Program for gifted middle schoolers and advised dual-enrolled students at WMU.

Luke Steinman was the Graduate Assistant for Western Michigan University's (WMU) Office of Pre-College Programming and Program Coordinator for the office's K-12 Tutoring and Mentoring Services. Luke earned his master's degree in Clinical Mental Health Counseling from WMU and is currently working on his doctorate degree in Counseling Psychology at the University of Northern Colorado.

REFERENCES

American Association of Collegiate Registrars and Admissions Officers. (2018). Pre-college programs report - March 60-second survey 2018. Retrieved January 14, 2019 from https://www.aacrao.org/research-publications/research/admissions-reports/pre-college-programs-report---march-60-second-survey-2018

Basken, P. (2018, Nov. 9). US university merger with pre-college partner offers new model. *Times Higher Education*, (2383), 15.

Brewer, E. W., & McMahan Landers, J. (2005). A longitudinal study of the talent search program. *Journal of Career Development, 31*(3), 195–208. doi:10.1177/089484530503100304

Clasen, D. R. (2006). Project STREAM: A 13-year follow-up of a pre-college program for middle-and high-school underrepresented gifted. *Roeper Review, 29*(1), 55–63. doi:10.1080/02783190609554385

Glennie, E. J., Dalton, B. W., & Knapp, L. G. (2015). The influence of pre-college access programs on postsecondary enrollment and persistence. *Educational Policy, 29*(7), 963–983. doi:10.1177/0895904814531647

Gullatt, Y., & Jan, W. (2003). *How do pre-collegiate academic outreach programs impact college-going among underrepresented students?* Boston, MA: The Pathways to College Network. Retrieved from http://citeseerx.ist.psu.edu/viewdoc/download?doi=10.1.1.483.7094&rep=rep1&type=pdf

Hicks, T. (2005, Winter). Assessing the academic, personal and social experiences of pre-college students. *National Association of College Admissions Directors and Counselors Journal, 186*, 19–24. Retrieved from https://files.eric.ed.gov/fulltext/EJ682486.pdf

Horn, L. J., & Chen, X. (1998). *Toward resiliency: At-risk students who make it to college.* Washington, DC: U.S. Dept. of Education, Office of Educational Research and Improvement.

Mattson, C. E. (2007, Summer). Beyond admission: Understanding pre-college variables and the success of at-risk students. *Journal of College Admission, 196*, 8–13. Retrieved from https://files.eric.ed.gov/fulltext/EJ783950.pdf

Partridge, C. E. (2016). *The impact of TRIO upward bound program participation on student outcomes: TRIO upward bound case study* (Doctoral dissertation, University of Cincinnati). Retrieved from http://rave.ohiolink.edu/etdc/view?acc_num=ucin1457426206

Perna, L. W., & Swail, W. S. (2001). Pre-college outreach and early intervention. *Thought & Action, 17*(1), 99–110. Retrieved from http://repository.upenn.edu/gse_pubs/287

Quinn, A. (2015). *A case study of an Upward Bound program director at a midwestern university* (Doctoral dissertation). Available from ERIC (ED567930).

Raines, J. M. (2012). FirstSTEP: A preliminary review of the effects of a summer bridge program on pre-college STEM majors. *Journal of STEM Education, 13*(1), 22–29.

Seftor, N. S., Mamun, A., & Schirm, A. (2009). The impacts of regular Upward Bound on postsecondary outcomes 7-9 years after scheduled high school graduation. Washington, DC: U.S. Department of Education. Available from ERIC (ED505850).

Sheth, S., & Tremblay, C. (2018, February). *Pre-college programming model: 25 dimensions*. Preliminary report.

Standing, K., Judkins, D., Keller, B., & Shimshak, A. (2008). *Early outcomes of the GEAR UP Program: Final report*. Washington, DC: U.S. Department of Education. Retrieved from https://www2.ed.gov/rschstat/eval/highered/gearup/early-outcomes.pdf

Swail, W. S., & Perna, L. W. (2002). Pre-college outreach programs: A national perspective. In W. G. Tierney & L. S. Hagedorn (Eds.), *Increasing access to college: Extending possibilities for all students* (pp. 15–34). Albany, NY: State University of New York Press. Retrieved from http://www.sunypress.edu/pdf/60559.pdf.

Swail, W. S., Quinn, K., Landis, K., & Fung, M. (2012, April). A blueprint for success: Case studies of successful college outreach programs. Washington, DC: Educational Policy Institute.

U.S. Department of Education. (n.d.) *Gaining early awareness and readiness for undergraduate programs (GEAR UP): Purpose*. Retrieved from https://www2.ed.gov/programs/gearup/index.html

U.S. Department of Education. (n.d.) *Talent search program: Purpose.* Retrieved from www2.ed.gov/programs/triotalent/index.html

Venezia, A., & Jaeger, L. (2013). Transitions from high school to college. *The Future of Children, 23*(1), 117–136. doi:10.2307/23409491

Chapter 14

Recommendations and Implications for the Future

By Susan Sheth, Ph.D., Michigan State University
and Christopher W. Tremblay, Ed.D.,
Michigan College Access Network

This first-of-a-kind publication summarizing the state of the current and growing pre-college programming field in higher education will now explore where we see this area going in the near future. These 12 expected trends will impact the field in some form or another:

Continued growth and development

Given what we have observed among American colleges and universities in the last decade, as they have grown pre-college programs and established offices/divisions for these programs, we expect this trend to continue. Pre-college programs are a natural fit to the evolving enhancement of a college's enrollment pipeline. As the U.S. and states continue to be laser focused on establishing and meeting postsecondary attainment goals and expanding access, pre-college programs have a role to play in meeting those goals.

Professionalization of the pre-college programming field

With the potential growth of pre-college programs comes the need for an expansion of professional development for individuals and leaders working in this landscape. The recent work of the newly named "Association for Pre-College Program Directors" is indicative of where this is headed. Formalizing this group of individuals brings additional recognition to this important work and enables pre-college programming professionals the opportunity to learn and mentor the next generation of leaders working in this space.

Strategic Enrollment Management (SEM) practices

We have begun to see a growing intersection of pre-college programming and strategic enrollment management (SEM). For example, Carnegie Mellon University (CMU) posted an "Assistant Director for Pre-College Enrollment Management" position in 2019, signaling how enrollment management practices are now being used in the pre-college context. This demonstrates the changing expectations for pre-college professionals. This role at CMU incorporates these aspects of enrollment management: financial aid, marketing, admissions, recruitment, and branding. We expect to see more colleges and universities connecting SEM and pre-college, especially since it connects well with a college's enrollment pipeline development plan. Some pre-college programs are even housed in Divisions of Enrollment Management for this very reason.

Centralization of pre-college programs

For decades, many pre-college programs on college campuses operated in silos. It was not uncommon for a faculty member to create a program based on a need or academic interest. As more departments on a college campus are interested in offering pre-college programs, this will require more collaboration and centralization. We expect to see divisions/units centered around pre-college programming developing in the coming years. This just needs like a natural progression for streamlining processes and ensuring programs are 100% compliant.

Focus on compliance

There is no question that recent incidents with minors have brought unfortunate visibility to pre-college programs. However, there have been many lessons learned from these real-life case studies. The creation of the Higher Education Protection Network (HEPNet) is an example of the creation of support, resources and conversation to ensure that minors are protected on every campus across the country. We expect to see the continued establishment of child protection roles and compliance offices on campuses, especially where there are many pre-college programs. We cannot emphasize the important nature of compliance. Roles with titles like Youth Safety and Compliance Manager will be added to protect both children and the colleges. Furthermore, colleges will be developing and revising their "minors on campus" policies and training pre-college professionals at a greater extent than we have ever seen in the past.

Emphasis on 21st Century Skills

Historically, many pre-college programs offered by colleges and universities have centered around an academic topic or subject. Looking ahead, there will be an emphasis on programs that emphasize and teach 21st century skills (see table below).

Table 1. 21st Century Skills

Critical Thinking	Creativity	Collaboration	Communication
Information Literacy	Media Literacy	Technology Literacy	Flexibility
Leadership	Initiative	Productivity	Social Skills

Source: aeseducation.com/career-readiness/what-are-21st-century-skills

These skills align with how K-12 leaders are targeting their curriculums and how college-level generation education programs are shifting their focus.

Dimensions as a best practices tool

Our vision for the 25 Dimensions introduced in Chapter 5 is for them to become the gold standard for benchmarking a highly effective pre-college programming operation. The formalization and adoption of this tool in the field would provide a common language for standards and could be used for the potential development of Council for the Advancement of Standards around pre-college programming, beyond what is currently documented for TRIO and College Access Programs.

Continued commitment to access and inclusion

Just like colleges and universities are laser-focused on increasing access, inclusion and success among current college students, pre-college programs are poised to become role models for expanding access and offering an inclusive environment for youth. Just look at the Queer Academics and Activism Program at Brandeis University (See Chapter 12) as one example. Pre-college programs around the theme of first-generation college students is likely around the corner.

Generation "Alpha"

Pre-college programs are currently serving students in Generation Z, but the next generation, being dubbed "Generation Alpha," was born after 2010, which means they will soon start entering (or already have) our pre-college programs, depending on what age/grade level your programs begin. Generation Alpha are the children of millennials and will be born from 2010 to 2025. That means they will definitely be in our pre-college programs from 2022 up to 2043. Mark McCrindle is a social researcher from Australia who coined the phrase "Generation Alpha" and he states, "Generation Alpha will be the most formally educated generation ever, the most technology-supplied generation ever, and globally the wealthiest generation ever" (Pasquarelli & Schultz, 2019, n.p.). This means that pre-college programs will need to keep up with the pace of these education levels, incorporate technology where it currently is not and meet the needs of their higher expectations. Simultaneously, this might mean using pre-college programs for students to "unplug" from technology and demonstrating to them how learning happens even without technology.

Increase of internal and external partners
Establishing internal partners beyond just support from the university administration can help make or break a pre-college program. Working with faculty and staff on campus is a necessity, but looking beyond into some new partnerships with departments like grants or development can aid in funding the programs. Some pre-college programs have worked with development colleagues to create endowment funds that provide annual financial support for programming or student scholarships. External partners can bring the career aspect of a program to create that more co-op style of learning for students. Corporations, hospitals and local school districts as partners will become stronger and more valuable for maximizing program offerings.

Broadening the age focus
The majority of pre-college programs created their initial programs to accommodate high school students, and eventually middle school students, but as parents, students and teachers have become more aware of the benefits and unique opportunities for elementary students, more and

more universities are expanding their focus on younger students for various reasons. Widening the age focus to cover even Pre-K-12 can create automatic internal feeder programs for the university as well as encourage expansion to subjects and disciplines beyond the typical day school regimes. In addition, these elementary grade level pre-college programs can feed students into programming that follows at the middle and high school level.

Need for more research

There is no question that we need to know more about what is effective among pre-college programs and their operations. This is largely an untapped space with so much potential. The growth of pre-college programs creates more opportunities to measure this phenomenon. We recommend that every practitioner consider how they can contribute to this emerging body of literature so we can continue to learn from each other. Opportunities for pre-college research includes impact of programs, the role in college decision-making, and the implication for degree attainment, for example. Research conducted in the coming years will impact the future practices of this field.

Concluding thoughts

We hope this book is just the beginning of documenting the evolving nature of the pre-college programming field. We look forward to seeing what is next for this area in American higher education. This is more than a trend; the movement will broaden and will continue to provide new and unique opportunities for students in their future pursuit of higher education.

REFERENCE

Pasquarelli, A., & Schultz, E. J. (January 22, 2019). Move over Gen Z, Generation Alpha is the one to watch. Retrieved online at adage.com/article/cmo-strategy/move-gen-z-generation-alpha-watch/316314

Professional Development in Pre-College Programming

National Pre-College and Youth Outreach Programming Pre-Conference Workshop
Hosted by the Engagement Scholarship Consortium
Held annually in September
engagementscholarship.org

Higher Education Protection Network (HEPNet) Conference
Annual Conference
Held in October
higheredprotection.org/conference

Association for Pre-College Program Directors
Annual Conference
Held in the Fall
Location rotates annually

Michigan Pre-College and Youth Outreach Conference
Annual Conference
(Location rotates among state universities)
michiganpcc.org

Contact Us

To reach the co-editors of this book, e-mail us at precollegebook@gmail.com

Index

business, 15, 87, 88
calendar, 54, 56
Camps on Campus, 123
campus culture, 146
campus partners, 37, 42, 155
campus-based, 12, 16
campus-wide approach, 22
career counseling, 170
career development, 169
career exploration, 14, 170
career paths, 1
career ready, 174
career shadowing opportunities, 2
career-based outreach, 169
Carnegie Mellon University, vii, 91, 92,
    108, 180
central administrator, 19
central office, 54
central organizational support, 18
central repository, 119, 120
centralization, 18, 22, 180
centralized repository, 54
child abuse, 109, 110, 114, 119, 120
child neglect, 109
Child Online Privacy Protection Act
    (COPPA), 110, 111, 122
child pornography, 109
Child Protection Improvements Act
    (CPIA), 110, 111, 122
child protection services, 117
Children's Online Privacy Protection Act
    (COPPA), 54
civil rights law, 112
class, 11, 85, 104, 105, 151
Clemson University, 33
coaching, 146
collaboration, 19, 20, 34, 46, 67, 87, 167,
    181
collaborative practices, 12
collective understanding, 151
college access, 11, 12, 13, 15, 16, 17, 22,
    31, 55, 65, 67, 70, 71, 72, 164, 166,
    175
College Access Programs, 6, 7, 10, 66,
    72, 182
college admissions (see also
    admission), 14, 69, 75, 84, 164
college attendance, 163
College Board, 167
college campuses, 5, 14, 23, 171
college choice, 154
college credit, 2, 82, 97, 104
college degree, 1, 11, 146, 165
college education, 13, 89, 107
college enrollment, 21, 23, 65, 67, 69, 70,
    72, 165, 169, 174

college enrollment gap, 65
college enrollment rates, 65
college entrance exam assistance, 14
college expectations, 167
college exposure, 170
college life, 1, 38, 167
college norms, 92, 94, 95
college participation, 6
college persistence, 174
college preparation, 26, 66, 67, 73
college readiness, 7, 38, 73, 74, 75, 169,
    170
college-going culture, 166
college-going path, 15
Collins, Nick, 31
Columbia College, 30
communication tools, 54
communication/communications, v, 3,
    10, 15, 22, 54, 61, 62, 99, 181
communities, 12, 17, 18, 27, 73, 75, 151,
    152
community, 12, 14, 16, 17, 18, 19, 20, 23,
    25, 26, 38, 40, 44, 55, 71, 72, 73, 74,
    81, 85, 89, 107, 121, 149, 152, 153,
    154, 155, 156, 171, 173, 174
community of practice, 18, 19, 20
community organizations, 20, 55, 56
community-based, 16
commuter, 15, 37, 39
competition, 9, 45, 46, 174
completion, 7, 8, 71, 137, 159, 164, 170,
    173
compliance, 34, 42, 54, 60, 61, 109, 112,
    120, 172, 181
composition, 13, 85
comprehensive, 5, 47, 48, 55, 119, 158,
    172
Conference on Youth Programs in
    Higher Education, 32
confidence, 1, 68, 92, 142
consent forms, 54
content, 16, 24
continuing education, 18, 40
coordination, 18, 56, 58
Cornell University, 30
corporations, 183
Council for Opportunity in Education
    (COE), 167
Council for the Advancement of
    Standards (CAS), 6, 10, 60, 182
counseling, 14, 68, 69, 170
course registration, 41
courses, 8, 37, 40, 47, 48, 68, 74, 84, 93,
    94, 95, 97, 104, 142, 175
creativity, 56, 68, 181
criminal background check, 110

investment, 17, 18, 19, 20, 21, 22, 23, 71, 72, 79, 86, 169
Ithaca College, 30
Johns Hopkins University, 30, 137
K-12 classroom knowledge, 2
K-12 education, 21, 22, 66
K-12 leaders, 182
K-12 school participants, 29, 171
K-12 students, 1, 8, 12, 55, 135, 140
Kansas City, Missouri, 32
Kellogg Commission on the Future of State and Land-Grant Universities, 12, 25
knowledge about college, 166
knowledge-based economy, 11, 12
Kolb, David, 91, 92, 94, 95, 99, 100, 105
laboratory science, 13
language, 42, 47, 92, 151, 154
laws, 53, 54, 84, 98, 109, 110, 112, 118, 122, 123, 156
lawsuit, 113, 116
leadership, vi, 9, 17, 49, 56, 61, 68, 73, 74, 80, 129, 137, 150, 151, 158, 164, 168, 174, 175, 181
learning, v, 1, 12, 24, 25, 43, 56, 57, 59, 68, 75, 91, 92, 93, 94, 95, 97, 99, 100, 101, 102, 103, 106, 107, 108, 128, 131, 132, 133, 134, 137, 143, 144, 145, 149, 183
lectures, 152, 157, 158, 159, 160
lessons learned, 37, 48, 173
LGBTQIA+ activism, 158
LGBTQIA+ community, 157, 158
LGBTQIA+ focus, 158
LGBTQIA+ issues, 152, 158
LGBTQIA+ teens, 152
library, 43, 157
lifelong learning, 56
listserv, 31
literature, 13
local school districts, 131, 183
logic modeling, 22
longitudinal data, 21, 70, 72
long-term, 15, 39, 68, 72, 79, 86, 169
Louis Stokes Alliance for Minority Participation Program (LSAMP), 166
low-income, 13, 14, 65, 66, 67, 68, 69, 71, 73, 75, 164, 168, 169
low-income students, 13, 54, 66, 67, 68, 164
majors, 17, 68, 153, 177
maltreatment, 109
management, 43, 47, 49, 57, 85, 88, 103, 115, 117, 118, 119, 121, 122, 135, 173
management by walking around, 121
marginalization, 142, 144, 151

marital, 53
marketing, 31, 41, 45, 48, 83, 84, 85, 86, 87, 88, 180
Massachusetts Institute of Technology, 30
math and science, 169
mathematics, 13, 15, 175
McCrindle, Mark, 183
media literacy, 181
media releases, 54
medical authorization forms, 112
medical management, 109, 115
medical treatment, 54
men, 65
mentor/mentoring/mentorship, 14, 68, 74, 75, 128, 136, 157, 164, 170, 180
Michigan College Access Network, vi, vii, 10, 35, 63
Michigan Pre-College and Youth Outreach Conference, 10, 31, 35, 63, 187
Michigan State University, vii, 1, 9, 11, 17, 24, 31, 53, 136
middle school students, v, 73, 75, 183
minority students, 15, 71
minors, 39, 40, 42, 44, 45, 54, 84, 93, 109, 111, 112, 113, 114, 116, 118, 119, 120, 121, 123, 124, 125, 136, 181
Minors on Campus conference, 32
mission, 1, 6, 7, 11, 30, 37, 38, 45, 46, 47, 48, 56, 57, 59, 80, 127, 144, 149, 150, 167, 173
mixed age groups, 114
molestation, 110
motivation, 17, 22, 68, 167, 168
MSU College of Veterinary Medicine, 133
multidisciplinary efforts, 20
music, 92
Nassar, Larry, 109, 119
National Association of College and University Attorneys (NACUA), 111
National Center for Education Statistics, 65
National Collaborative for the Study of University Engagement, 24
National Educational Longitudinal Study (NELS), 165
National High School Game Academy, 93
national laws and regulations, 109, 122
National Student Clearinghouse (NSC), 21, 55
nationality, 53, 140
neglect, 110, 114, 117, 119, 120, 122
networking, 20

53249304R00116

Made in the USA
Lexington, KY
27 September 2019